# KEEP GOING TO SUCCEED ALWAYS

# PERSISTENCE BEATS INTELLIGENCE FOR SUCCESS

**Gautam Sharma**

**and**

**Shormistha  Chatterjee**

**( Dedicated to valued readers)**

# COPYRIGHT

# Table of Contents

INTRODUCTION Would you like to get what you want in life every time? Become more a happy long term, be more youthful with a healthy bodyand a sharp mind , keep joyous relationships, have satisfying work and income, enjoy big houses, cars, and vacations? Ever wondered how so many people are successful and some have lead extraordinary lives-as far as creating history and benefiting mankind at large? Think for a moment about the greatest people overcenturies There is a distinct, common attribute that has made many men and women extremely successful and renowned over centuries and across continents. From Alexander the Great( 356 BC ) to Cleopatra, Genghis Khan, Michael Angelo, Joan of Arc, Mahatma Gandhi, Winston Churchill, Marie Curie, Einstein, Thomas Edison, Benjamin Franklin to present day outstanding people as Bill Gates, Warren Buffet, some other billionaires and world leaders. It's just not mental or physical prowess, talents, education, training or good luck that worked for them. The outstanding common attribute among all successful and extraordinary people of excellence across all space and time has been the quality of persistence, attitude, and motivation.

It's been about keeping on going towards their goals in the face of denials, obstacles, failures, and opposition. The unstoppable keep on going; whatever the odds, slowdowns or roadblocks and they achieve success, victory, and fame. This book will help you gain the magic of persistence, motivation and determined attitude. You can also become very persistent and super successful. Let us look at what it is and why it is so important.

Persistence is the attitude and the personality trait to continue with determination on a set course of action to overcome difficulties, failures or opposition until the required goals are achieved.

There are several reasons why persistence is important:

 1. 1. It shows that you are ambitious and that

you have high goals and objectives to achieve. If you want to go to some places, you will have reason to find ways to reach there.

2. 2. Your ambition and subsequent drive make you stand out and make others notice your determined, dominant personality.

3. 3. Persistence makes you garner skills, experiences, and abilities. The process of working harder to overcome failure helps you acquire new, peripheral skills or hone onto the current ones.

4. Working harder helps build inner strength and stamina. The determination to think and work is to keep going on doing activities methodically and consistently going step by step doing activities that are required for your goals. Reasons Why Persistence is the Key to Success?

In simple words, persistence means the attitude and personality trait of working hard and trying again and again until complete success is achieved.

Here is why persistence is the key to success and why you should develop it as a vital personality trait.

1. Persistence makes you an expert

You may not be good at doing something for the first time but you will get better at it when you keep trying for the second time, third time and so on. With persistence, you will continue to do the same thing over and over again until you achieve complete success. This will make you an expert in whatever task you are doing.

2. Being persistent will motivate you to try harder. Being persistent means you will keep trying again and again. With every attempt, you will inch closer to success. It will motivate you to put more effort to get closer to your goals when you see that there is an actual difference between where you stand right now, and your previous effort. Self-motivation is an important aspect of being successful.

3. Persistence is a sign of being ambitious.

Only those people who are highly ambitious can incorporate persistence into every aspect, every little thing that they do in their daily lives. When you keep attempting something with persistence, everyone around you will look at you as an ambitious person. It will build a positive personality image for you, a key in shaping the outlook of a successful persona.

4. Persistence will set a good example to your associates and peers.

A reason why persistence is the key to success especially in workplaces is the reason your colleagues and subordinates will be inspired by your level of persistence. When they see you achieving your goals with determined persistence, they too will try to imitate this trait. This will result in an overall boost in productivity and efficiency for your team, making persistence a highly regarded personality trait in any workplace.

5. Persistence teaches you the value of success

Are you under the false notion that success can be achieved easily by manipulative tactics? Do you think that success can be easily bought? Do you think that success comes with just a little bit of effort? If you have these untrue thoughts in your head, persistence will teach you that success is not that easy to achieve. As you keep attempting to achieve a goal over and over again, you will understand the true value of success. It will enlighten you about the amount of hard work and dedication required to make something happen, preparing you to give your best shot at everything in life if you want to be successful.

## 6. Persistence will help you gain experience

Being persistent means getting up after a failure, learning from your mistakes and trying again. This whole process will help you gain experience, which is vital if you want all-rounded success. The Multiple numbers of attempts at the same thing will help you find out the things that can go wrong, the things that are crucial to a process or the things that are not required at all. This experience, which was a result of persistence, will teach you stuff that books and procedure manuals don't.

## 7. Persistence will make you aware of your weakness

**To be successful, you need to be aware of your weaknesses and your faults. Your weaknesses will only be exposed when you analyze your failures and try to find out the things you lack to accomplish something. This is only possible if you are mentally prepared to accept failure, try again, fail again and keep trying until you iron out all your weaknesses to finally succeed. This is why being persistent is the key to success. The most effective words for a lifetime of achievement, success, fun, happiness, joy, and fulfillment: "Keep going. Keep going towards the light, your goals, towards the promise of so much goodness that awaits you. With joyous feelings, hope in your heart, and a song on your lips keep going and receiving achievements, success, love, friendships, fame, fortunes and all else you had imagined. See the pure white light beckoning you, find your path through**

**whatever comes in the way and keep going.**

**Persistence-The State of Mind**

Success is something we all wish for, isn't it? Undeniably, those who attain great things are those who don't know when to give up. Whether you wish to achieve something or want to lose a few pounds or any goal that you are willing to succeed in, you need to be strong and persistent. Indeed the most successful people in the world have the key quality of perseverance which makes them assume impossible actions to be possible. How many of you can claim with confidence that you have applied persistence and consistency in your everyday life with some measure of success? I think the majority of us dream of incredible things but just lack persistence or the willpower, to follow through to accomplishment. People give up too soon as they have the wrong expectations of themselves and the results. They expect the mode to be easy, and they are amazed when they find the reality to be contradictory. Their enthusiasm quickly melts and they quit. What does being willpower and persistent mean? It is a cliche to simply say "don't give up".

One of the best illustrations persistence is the state of mind and sustained effort necessary to induce faith. In other words, it exemplifies that determination mixed with Persistence backed by the desire makes a strong tool to ensure the achievement of the goals". The meaning of the term persistence is the quality that allows an individual to continue doing things even if it is tricky or opposed by other people. This is not something someone does with external goals; however, it is something someone does internally. Perhaps we all are aware of the fact that in the face of pain, anguish, suffering, and defeat; it may not be easy to stay persistent. In simple words, persistence means the personality and attitude trait of working harder and harder and trying again and again until success is achieved. Abraham Lincoln is a leading example of persistence and strong willpower in action. Known as one of the renowned presidents in history, Abraham lost 8 elections before he, in the end, became president. He also lost his fortune when he starts losing his business twice and could have chalked himself up to being a loser, but he didn't. However, he didn't lack his determination and believed he could achieve his dreams. If you are passionate about something, chances are you're determined to move towards that activity or thing. It is the quality that motivates people to do things however difficult or unpopular they may be.

## *Chapter One*

### *Keep going until you are successful*

The conventional definition of persistence is: "not letting go or refusing to give up; persevering persistently; firm or obstinate continuation in a course of action in spite of trouble or opposition." It is a developed state of mind much like grit. It is the trademark of achievements since persistent persons push through difficulty, anguish, and pain which refers to the setbacks and roadblocks when pursuing an objective. As the significant component of self-discipline, determination and persistence also provide its own inspiration and motivation. You become more enthusiastic to do something incredibly when your activities started showing results. For instance, when you want to lose all those extra pounds and start exercise and to workout, you will be more enthused when you lost 20-25 lbs and your present wardrobe starts fitting loose Persistence can conquer almost any challenge. When you turn your mind to something and are eager to do everything it takes, by putting in the time and adjusting your plan to get there, you will eventually know the supremacy and power of determination. Some of the major factors or symptoms of lack of persistence are indecision, not being clear in what you want, lack of proper planning, weak desire, fear of criticism, feeling of insignificance and lack of going all out. You may not be fine at doing something for the first time but you will get better and better at it when you keep trying and believe in yourself for the second time, third time and so on. With persistence and consistency, you will continue to do the similar thing over and over again until you accomplish complete success. This will make you a proficient in whatever job you are doing. You have to believe that your victory is guaranteed and no obstacle will stand your way.

Billionaires and political leaders had failed several times and have thought of giving up college but they finally come out ahead as big winners. Edison also made more than 10 thousand experiments before he accomplishes something in making the first talking machine. As the primary factor of self-discipline, persistence also provides its own motivation. You become enthusiastic to do something when your actions started showing great performance and results. Courageous persistence is the main factor than any other that can promise success. And success is somewhat we all want, isn't it? But to be victorious takes persistence. Whether you want to lose your extra fat, get an A in a class, or any goal that you want to succeed in, you need to be persistent. It is the difference between a successful result and a failed one due to giving up.

Perseverance has other names — determination, persistence, a can-do attitude. When getting starting on your vision for success, first and foremost you need to identify your desires and wants. It is when you know the way; you can get a source for inspiration and keep yourself encouraged next, figure out how to achieve what you want? This makes it easier to attain it. Make your objectives actionable every day and follow through. All your objective-setting and planning will go to waste if you won't be able to build up discipline and good habits. Be positive in your work that you will attain what you want. Perseverance separates the losers from the winners. Those who persevere understand that luck is something only failures believe in. Success in life depends on your motivation to never give up, even when the reward is delayed.

How to stay persistent?

Like all states of mind, persistence is based upon specific causes. Take a piece of paper and write down a life goal, what you desire, and answer the questions; what is your definite purpose. Knowing what one longing for is the former and, perhaps, the most important step toward the growth of persistence. Strong motive forces can easily overcome many hurdles of our life. Similar questions like why do you want to accomplish this goal? How will it profit you and the more essential, how will it benefit others? In order to survive your purpose, you have to keep the focus on why you want this purpose/ goal or what the positive results will be in your life? We do have to keep in our mind that our purpose in this world is also to add value to others. If your wishes focus on your own gratification you will sooner or later fail or die a lonely miserable life.

All successful people who have attained great things in their life did so through both willpower and persistence. Even when they failed, they got encouragement and kept going. But we all know that staying determined and persistent is difficult. In any conversation of the qualities of the most successful people, it is always declared that Persistence is one of the, most significant factors in success. Major success rarely comes easily or without an enormous deal of attempt. Often the only distinction between those who succeed and those who do not is the capacity to keep going long after the break has dropped out. It is comparatively easy to persist when things are going smoothly and we see progress, however, great persistent people have found several means to keep going in spite of major setbacks and a lack of confirmation that they are driving near toward their goals.

Some of the significant things that persistent people have in common that keep them moving on long after so many people have given up:

## Visualization for success

Persistent people have a vision or goal in mind that encourages and drives them. They are often visionaries and dreamers who see their lives as having a high purpose than simply just spending their life. Their vision is deeply entrenched, and they concentrate on it continuously and with great energy and the state of mind. They often think of this dream first thing when they wake up and the last thing prior to they go to bed. Accomplishing this goal becomes the crucial and focal point of their life and they dedicate a major portion of their time and energies towards attaining it.

- ## Unshakable self-confidence, self-belief

Those persons who defeat the hurdles and accomplish greatly are often illustrated as "marching to the beat of their own drummer."

Persistence people know what they wish for and are seldom swayed by the view of the masses. To have the perfect intelligence of who they really are, allows the persistent to carry on without being seriously affected by what others think of them or, being appreciated, or being understood by those around them. At the same time as that inner confidence gets shaken, but never gets shattered and continuously acts as a source of courage and strength.

- **Inherent passion to succeed**

There are so many inspiring Entrepreneur and Industrialists who always speak, "If you really desire to do something, you will surely discover a way. If you do not, you will find an excuse." Persistent people never look for any excuse. What keeps persistent people going is their potent level of desire. Repeated failures, losing periods and dead ends, when it seems like no progress is being made, often come before some breakthroughs happen. Persistent people with high will-power have the intensity, state of mind, and inner energy to keep them motivated and going through these hard-hitting times.

## • Talent to Adjust and Acclimatize

Persistent people have the capacity to acclimatize and adapt their action plan. They do not stubbornly persevere in the face of indication that their plan is not running but look for enhanced ways that will increase their probability of success. The motivated and persistent see their life journey as a bunch of dead ends, adjustments, and deviations, but have total faith they will reach their final objective. They are not attached to their ego and are rapidly willing to admit when something is not working. In addition, they are fast to adopt the fresh ideas of others that have been shown to work well.

## • Key success habits

As someone truly said, "Motivation is what gets you going ahead. Habit is what keeps you going."Highly persistent people know it is very tricky to stay constantly motivated, chiefly during hard and the most difficult times and when it appears that no development is being made. They have come to rely upon their self-developing and discipline habits they can count on to carry on the path toward their ultimate goals. They believe the results of the hard work they make today may not be seen for a longer time, but they strongly believe that every single thing they do will count toward their end results.

- **Commitment to acquire new skills**

Persistent people understand the worth of any objective and reaching will take attempt, time, and constantly learning new skills and thoughts patterns. They welcome fresh ideas and change and continue searching for means they can incorporate these into their lives. Ongoing learning is seen as part of a continuous process through which the highly persistent continually expand the range of tools that they have to work with. Naturally curious type persons not only see learning as a way to reach their objectives more quickly, but they also see self-learning as a way of life. Learning and constant growth do not end at a certain age or phase of life, but they are the spirit of life itself, and thus never-ending.

- **Role models as mentors and motivators**

While it may come into sight that highly persistent people act without help and don't require any person, most have carefully chosen peoples they follow and admire. These can be individuals who are truly involved in their lives as guides or they can be figures who they have read about and who have extremely impacted them. Such people are often misunderstood on the grounds that they can make those around them feel uncomfortable. The ingrained models assist motivated persons to maintain and motivate themselves in an atmosphere that is not always kind and supportive.

The winners' circle defines persistence as refusing to give up when faced with opposition or hardship. It could be expressed as simply as trying again and again until you keep scoring at sports, maintaining relationships or succeeding at work or businesses. The greatness that you have, the greatness of the condition, is not calculated by what is accomplished. It is calculated exactly by how many times you pick yourself up and try to accomplish something. Among all of the values and morals we can have, it seems persistence is the consistent element in most people who thrive and succeed, no matter what they are succeeding at. We all seem to understand or know that all popular personalities have persistence in huge quantities. They have to keep their mind strong, keeping the boundaries of patience in order to attain the new records. Yet, you can see persistence all over the place you look, even for the job you get paid to do, so there ought to be something incredible to it. If in case you are evaluating what amount of struggle it would take to give your career a boost up, you might come across in the direction of your own persistence. You need to be clear about what you are determined to achieve. What is the result you are in the hunt for? If you need to gather knowledge or resources, then go get them. Once you have your objective, your plan, and the resources, then goes after it with dedication and enthusiasm. Stay focused every day until you get the outcomes you defined. It is also OK to occasionally get propped up by close relatives, family or friends to keep the required attitude that comes with persistence. Persistence is not about the trouble-free road, even though few people make attaining success look easy. Persistence is about systematic and continued to do something even when there is a good reason to give up. Persistence is about the basic confidence of knowing your vision is the right thing to pursue.

## Make persistence a lifelong habit

Another most significant piece to having the higher persistence level is having support. Sometimes when it came to the list of things we wanted to accomplish personally, having a team of people who were above or on your level made you want to persevere and keep going for your aspirations. It is healthy and nice to have a supportive team like family, close friends, relatives, religion and particularly mentors that can be there beside you when you necessitate an additional boost up of motivation. Support from others is always advantageous, but not always simple to find. If you feel like you don't have a mentor or guide in your support team that you could, in fact, talk and sit down to about your aspirations, make an effort to find one, particularly one that has been where you are and who is at present where you are aspiring to go. There is no sense in having a support team that cannot bond and connect to your goals for the reason that they do not have any aspiring goals themselves. You need to evaluate your crowd cautiously and warily. Having a good imagination and thoughts also helps when it comes to persistence. When you can visualize and think about your "dream future" no matter what that might be, these visions every so often can get you through the harsh days. Do not let one failure in your journey of life to success dictate your motivation for the rest of the life. Each and every step is to bring you closer to your ideas and dreams, and when you can clearly notice your upcoming "dream future," you can fully fashion it under your own conditions.

Persistence in the provision of an ultimate crucial goal calls out numerous other virtues in you. You will push yourself to further than what is comfortable to achieve your chosen goal. Furthermore, you should know why you desire your goal in the first place. Plus, your way must be bigger than the difficulties and complications. The bigger the way the better the outcomes, Persistent people have a transparent goal or vision in mind that inspires and induces them. Reaching this ultimate goal becomes the central focal point of their life journey and they devote a larger percentage of their time toward reaching it. If we would like to succeed, we have to pay the price. And the way to success is long with a lot of hurdles and obstacles. No wonder most of the people stop at one point or another after running into the obstacle or barriers. Only the handful of people has this special quality to keep moving forward, and these are some people who succeed. Persistence is essential. Persistence is probably one of the most worthy and excellent characters a person can possess. It's the ability to be determined to accomplish something regardless of any obstructions and setbacks. Hence, arm yourself with the right state of mind and the right tactics to overcome failure. Perseverance or Persistence is mainly about the basic optimism of knowing your dream is the right thing to chase. In fact, there is no other way to succeed and achieve something huge but by developing persistence in your life, and here we would also share a few significant ways to develop it.

## Do you believe in persistence?

Aren't you? Persistence is being able to continue a human action until one has succeeded, like winning a race. When you start running, you keep on pushing yourself until you have crossed the finish line. For instance, in special education, having persistence in teaching a kid until he/she has reached their ultimate goal is like a race. You are persistent in helping them reach their destination and don't stop until they have reached their objective. People tend to hold on to their beliefs even when it seems that they should not. Persistence is the tendency to cling to one's initial belief even after receiving fresh information that dis-confirms or contradicts or the basis of that belief. Every single person has tried to change somebody's belief, only to have them obdurately remain unchanged. For example, you may have had such debates concerning the abortion, or evolution.

In the plethora of cases, resistance to challenges to belie is defensible and logical. For instance, if you have always done well in racing, getting the third position on some race should not lead you to abandon your belief that you are generally good in the race. However, in the handful of cases, people cling to beliefs that logically should be abandoned, or at least altered. There is overpowering evidence that smoking increases the probability of contracting cancer and that exposure to media violence heightens the likelihood of aggressive behavior. Even, some people strongly deny these scientific facts. People expend considerable mental energy to maintain their opinion when presented with facts that prove them wrong. They will concentrate on experiences that support their point of view merely will ignore any experiences, even their own, that give grounds that they are wrong. They will do the same thing with any other kinds of evidence as well.

## Types of Belief of Perseverance

There are three types of belief perseverance exist —1) social impressions 2) self-impressions, and 3) social theories. The first kind of belief consists of beliefs about the self, considering what one believes about his skills and abilities, including body image and social skills. The second type comprises one belief about specific others, for instance, a parent or best friend. The third type comprises mainly what one believes about how the world mainly works, comprising how people act, feel, interact and think. Social theory opinion can be either directly or indirectly learned which means that they can learn through experience as a member or they can be taught. In the first case, children inclined to learn what is expected of them and of others merely by observing and by being a participating member of society. They will learn what it means to be a daughter, a son, a woman, a man, and the behaviors that go with these different roles. In the second case, persons are taught what to believe. They may be taught by their parents or at school, at church.

When it comes to attaining your objectives or creating change in your life if perhaps won't be simple. You may have to struggle. It will likely take a longer time period than you expect. It is almost certain that you will have short-term failures and setbacks along the way. Particularly, when it involves developing new skills, forming a new resolution, creating new habits, or learning new concepts. Now, the good news, struggle, setbacks, battles, and short-term obstacles do not have to drain your motivation. They do not have to make you want to quit before you have put in enough effort and time to accomplish your goal. In fact, psychologists who study motivation and accomplishment say it could be just the opposite; as long as you adopt the right path and the right mindset. According to my raids of research through decades, there are two fundamental belief systems, also called as "mindsets," that evaluate how people respond to setbacks, struggle, obstacles, and failure when pursuing their goals. In one mindset, you are most likely to get discouraged and give up on your ultimate goal. In the other, you tend to embrace the battle and struggle, learn from the hardship or hurdles and keep moving forward to attain your goals– you persevere.

**The science of Persistence: Determined Mindset vs Growth Mindset**

What do you believe about human calibers, such as intelligence, talent, and creativeness? If you have adopted a "fixed mindset," you view them as traits that you are either born with, or not, and it is not much you can do to alter it. On the flip side, if you have adopted a "growth mindset," you see them as capacities that you can develop through determination, practice, education, and hard work.

How about character traits like grit, willpower, and self-discipline? With a fixed mindset, you believe attributes like these are mostly static and predetermined by your genes and fostering – either you have them or you do not. Through the lens of a growth mindset, you see them as malleable skills that you can prepare, gear up and strengthen over the course of your life (even science also proves this to be true).

In a fixed mindset, people believe their basic attributes, like their intelligence, ability, or talent, are just fixed traits. They spend their time on the piece of writing their intelligence or talent instead of developing them. They also accept the fact that talent alone creates success; without excessive effort. They are actually wrong. On the flip side, in a growth mindset, people believe that their most basic qualities can be developed through dedication, commitment, and hard work. This view creates a love of learning and a resilience that is necessary for great achievement. Virtually all great people have had these calibers. Teaching a growth mindset creates productivity and motivation in the worlds of education, business, and sports. It deepens relationships. When you read Mindset, you will see how.

## Fixed Mindset Weakens Your Dedication

Our mind is a meaning-making machine. Whether you are aware of it or not, you are continuously monitoring what is happening around you, understanding what it means and deciding what to do about it. This is apparently the significant procedure for your survival, but it is also the main driver of all your suffering – particularly when it is molded by the fixed mindset. When you struggle hardship or fail to attain your ultimate objectives, you make that mean something about yourself. In the fixed mindset, this mainly means you are simply not good enough, or that you for some reason do not have what it takes. For instance, have you ever thought or said things like: I'm not creative, I don't have any self-discipline, I have no talent, I'm not good with new technology, It's hard for me to lose the extra pound, I'm shy, I am not athletic, etc. It is healthy to acknowledge your limitations and recognize where you can be doing better in your life. But that's not what's happening in the fixed mindset. Remember, the fixed mindset believes that abilities and talent are mainly fixed and preset – either you have it, or don't. If you have, great. If not, why even why bother to try? You might as well give up, and keep move on to something simpler. Perhaps, this is not the kind of thinking that helped the big personalities like J.K. Rowling and Stephen King become bestselling authors. It is not the kind of thinking that creates motivation to persevere when the going gets tough.

**Growth Mindset Fortifies Your Motivation**

The growth mindset interprets failure and challenging situations much differently than the fixed mindset. Just remember, the core opinion of the growth mindset is that human powers and talents are malleable skills that you can set up and strengthen over the course of your life. The fixed mindset erroneously views your limitations as permanent. On the other hand, the growth mindset understands they are just a starting turning point – guiding stars that tell you where to spend your energy toward professional and personal development. The growth mindset is an antidote to defeatism. It interprets challenge & failure, not as a signal to throw in the towel, however, as a healthy and natural part of human growing and accomplishment.

This might sound like a good old-fashioned or outdated positive thinking, and maybe it is. The difference of opinion is these conclusions are based on 40 years of stringent, scientific research – more than hundreds of studies that all say similar facts. If you want to strengthen your motivation, accomplish your goals and lead a more fulfilling life, you are best served by a growth mindset. You now have a choice with regard to how you interpret struggle, failure, and setbacks. You can interpret it from a fixed mindset as proof that you are somehow not cut out to win. Or you can interpret it from a growth mindset as guidance for where to keep your focus on your efforts toward personal & professional development. Most persistence research on naive theories has focused on beliefs about people and how they feel, behave, think, and interact and other social theories. Examples include stereotypes about teenagers, Muslims, Asian Americans; beliefs about artists, lawyers, firefighters; even beliefs about the causes of poverty, violence or war.

Early belief perseverance studies tested whether individuals often truly cling to unfounded viewpoints more so than is logically justifiable. However, it is complex and tricky to specify just how much a given belief "should" modify in response to fresh and New Testament. One "C Grade" on a math test should not completely overwhelm other years of "A"s in other math classes, however, how much transform (if any) is warranted? There is one clear and apparent case in which researchers can state how much belief change should happen. That case is when the basis of a precise belief is totally dishonored or discredited. For instance, imagine that John tells Maria that the new team member is not very active. Maria may even meet and interact with the new member for several days before learning that John was actually speaking about a different new joiner. Because Maria knows that his initial belief about new member's intelligence was based on completely irrelevant information, Maria's impression about the new joiner should now be totally uninfluenced by John's initial statement. This, in essence, describes the debriefing paradigm, the primary technique used to study unwarranted belief perseverance. In the first belief perseverance revision using this way, partially half of the research participant members were led to suppose and believe that they had performed fine on a social perceptiveness task; the rest half were led to judge that they had performed badly. Afterward, all were told that their performance had been manipulated by the researcher to see how participant members take action and respond to failure or success. Participants were even shown the paper sheet that listed their name and whether they were thought to be given failure or success feedback. Later, participants had to guess how well they really did and foresee how well they would do in the future on this assigned task or job.

Logically, those in the initial failure and success situations should not differ in their self-beliefs about their future or actual performance on this social perceptiveness job, for the reason that early beliefs based on the fake feedback should revert to their normal level once it was exposed that the feedback was faked. Nevertheless, participants who received fake success feedback constantly believe that they were pretty good at this task, while those who received fake failure comment persistently believe that they were pretty bad at it. Other studies of social impressions and self-impressions have found parallel effects concerning distinct beliefs.

The initial study of social theory persistence used the same debriefing paradigm to find out whether fictitious info about the relation between the personality attribute "riskiness" and firefighter quality could create a persevere social theory. Though, after debriefing about the fictitious nature of the first information, participants at the start led to believe that risky people make finer firefighters and those initially led to believe that high-risk people make poorer firefighters persist in their initial beliefs. At least there are three psychological procedures underlie belief perseverance. One refers to use of the "availability heuristic" for deciding what is most liable to happen. When judging your own power at a specific task, you are likely to try to recollect memory how good you have done on similar tasks in the past, that is, how available (in memory) are past successful versus failures. However, whether you recall more failures or successes critically depends on galore factors, such as how memorable the several occasions were and how often you have actually thought about them, but not inevitably on how often you have failed or succeeded. The second activity concerns "illusory correlation," wherein one sees or remembers more confirmed cases and few disconfirming cases than really subsist. The third procedure concerns "data distortions," wherein disconfirming cases are neglected and confirming cases are inadvertent. For instance, if you are told that a new team member is rude, you are more likely to treat that individual in a way that invites rudeness or discourtesy and to forget instances of politeness. Research also has examined ways to belief perseverance. The most obvious answer, asking people to be unbiased, does not work, nevertheless, various techniques to reduce the problem. The most successful is to get the individual to imagine or explain how the other belief might be true. This De-biasing technique is referred to as the counter explanation.

## Varied Types

There are three extraordinary kinds of belief perseverance, viz.

**Social impressions**

**Self-impressions**

**Naive theories**

### Social Impressions

Social Impressions bring up to the beliefs that people have about others. These could be supported on a one-time, previous experience (either positive or negative) that people have about others and shape an opinion, which leads into forming an opinion. These can be formed with just about any individual.

### Self-impressions

Self-impressions mention to the beliefs that we harbor about ourselves. These have to do with our belief about our confidence, athletic skills, body image, academic inescapable, musical knowledge, and the like. This belief system considers both negative and positive beliefs. For instance, somebody might be a good public speaker, however, he/ she has a strong belief that he cannot speak in the public place, and it cannot be shaken in spite of people complimenting him. The mistaken belief like this one can have severe consequences and can lead to a skewed perspective of oneself. On the other hand, an exaggerated view of someone can also lead to problems.

**Naive Theories**

Such impressions are based on someone's belief about how the world works. Naive theories mostly correspond with social theories—the belief about folks, how they behave, think, and interact with others. Naive theories go on to comprise major stereotypes steeped in the society that has to do with the handful of issues about communities, religion, teen, professions, and other beliefs that may even comprise what gives rise to poorness, causes of war, and violence, and the like.

**Chapter Two**

**Keep going until you are successful**

Holding on to set beliefs and speculations based on unwarranted data and in the light of conflicting evidence, demonstrates that conviction persistence exists, as well as that our conviction framework isn't just shaped based on certainties and sensible data, however to an expansive degree on how we feel about ourselves, about others, and about other general theories and hypotheses. Despite the fact that this unwavering belief can help from numerous points of view, most different occasions, it shapes a boundary which keeps us from settling on the correct decisions. Illustration of a similar will be featured in the accompanying area.

**Examples**

**Positive Example-**You're a brilliant cook and individuals dependably compliment you on your dishes. Yet, on one specific event, you happen to burn the sandwich you're cooking; this does not imply that you're an awful cook or that you need to scrutinize your conviction about being a decent cook. For this situation, the belief perseverance has enabled you to restore your confidence in your cooking and continue.

**Negative Examples**-However, there are occasions when belief perseverance goes about as a hurdle. For instance, a man has met with 4 accidents during a span of a month, but, he keeps on trusting that he is a superb driver. Or then again suppose that your companion has been dating a person who treats her badly, and whilst everybody around her can see this and have been revealing to her the same, she basically declines to say a final breakup to him since she trusts he loves her as too, and he will change.

In the two instances, the individual does not take cognizance of anything that repudiates his/her belief system, which at that point negatively affects his life, since he can't take logical conclusion or judgment.


Why Persistence significant in our Life?

Persistence is the essences of accelerating your

prospects of being successful in a specific thing or accomplishing a specific objective, and it likewise can assist you with staying motivated and continue striving towards the one long haul objective you want to achieve. For instance, when you first started your company, you most likely had dreams of success and recognition. You were positive that sales were reaching to pour in, and you'd be busy creating a great deal of cash. When you truly operated your company, it most likely dawned upon you rather quickly that hopes, visions, and dreams alone weren't sufficient. Starting a business taught you that being a business owner isn't as simple as you once thought it might be. In fact, it's a great deal of labor with little reward gained at the outset. This is the reason why business failure rates are thus high. Folks merely cannot overcome the roadblocks and demands that accompany entrepreneurship.

The one word that may be used to describe businessperson who succeeds at business ownership is 'persistent'. You need to be persistent if you would like to be ready to sustain your business through the challenges and hurdles of entrepreneurship and sooner or later reap the rewards of a successful business. The truth is that Entrepreneurship comes with loads of ups and downs. Typically it feels as if you expertise a lot of downs than ups as you're within the early stages of business development. This is often once your mental attitude needs to stay optimistic and tough if you're getting to go through the hardships of constructing your business. If you're presently having a tough time in your business, you'd get advantage from reading some quotes regarding persistence. These quotes can assist you to understand that you simply aren't the sole one who has undergone troubles as a business owner. Others are through what you're presently going through and possibly abundantly worse. But, they still built successful businesses despite their hurdles as a result of they remained to persevere.

The definition of Persistence is once you are desperate to do one thing considerably and not permitting anyone or any troubles stop you for doing it. This definition couldn't be any length suitable which is what the beauty of determination is and why it's therefore vital for anyone to have. With zero determination, it can lead you to give up on the single thing that you just needed to try to due to the issue that you just faced with or what somebody else has same. Nobody ought to ever surrender on one thing that they really need to try to as a result of everybody can achieve something if they are willing to place in the work a strong mindset towards overcoming the particular challenge and overcoming people that disagree and create trouble and don't have your best interest to your life.

Why Persistence is significant than planning?

We are mysterious creatures. Anguish and hope can coexist and still create something astonishing. Perseverance is the ability to maintain action despite your feelings. It has a lot to do with your life's success and business success. It is considered as an omnipotent. An American politician Calvin Coolidge once stated "The slogan "press on" has solved and always will solve the troubles of the human race". Intelligence and ability cannot take the place of persistence. The worth of persistence comes from a visualization of the future that is so compelling you would give approx anything to make it factual or real. Persistence of action draws closer from the persistence of vision. When you are specifically clear about what you want in such a way that your vision does not change much, you will be more unfailing and persistent in your dealings. Hence, that consistency of action will produce consistency of outcomes. One favorite quote state that "no plan survives first contact with the enemy." We have learned this reality time and time again. Mike Tyson put it well when he stated, "Everybody has an arrangement until the point when they get punched in the face." Regular arranging is basic to maintain a business yet we find that readiness and steadiness are significantly more imperative that the most ideal marketable strategy. Clear emergency courses of action were basic for mission achievement.


Here are reasons that being well-prepared and persistent to tackle life's obstruction is significant than trying to manage things out of your control.

Things do not generally go as planned, thus be ready when the inevitable obstruction or hurdles stand in your way. Whether you are the team member of the big-giant corporation or an entrepreneur growing a start-up, you have probably noticed that plans can change, and change often. But the enterprise has to be well-structured to remain dynamic, robust and strong. Good leaders must continue focused on what lays ahead for foreseeing potential blockage and adjust accordingly. Experiencing letdown along your path to accomplishment does not mean you failed. Failure generally occurs when you allow those experiences cause you to give up. Planning does not ensure adaptability In the Teams, while doing fight dive training we had a saying, "Plan your dive, & dive your plan." Things can get confusing underwater in pitch blackness, however, when you start second guess yourself, it can snowball uncontrollable. That's why it is said, good old fashion common sense is also a great reserve and stand-in when your plan starts falling apart.

For companies, they must have robust financials,

nimble leadership, and a team with a shared sense of purpose. Planning does not identify unknowns. Persistence and obstinacy are what makes companies successful. The character is built during the third and fourth shots at attaining the goal. Not the first try. In trade, there are always myriads of things out of your control like the economy or your client's financial situations. But that's senseless reason to irritate and make kneejerk decisions. You just have to stay calm, cool and positive and try to keep moving. A great quote about persistence from Martin Luther King Jr. states that "If you can't fly you run if you can't run you walk if you can't walk your crawls. But no matter what, you keep moving forward."

Good plans are valueless without proper implementation. Plus flawless execution takes some practice. You can use up all the time in the world developing big plans for your business but if you do not brag the ability to perform on those plans you will surely fail. There also has to be buy-in across the board for organizations to be effectual at hitting their goals. Never discount the significance of having a proper plan and even better contingency strategies. But you need to keep in mind that if you spend proper time to make sure you have the capability to adapt as required, it won't feel like you are trying to steer a cruise ship when an iceberg placed in your pathway. It is perseverance that keeps you moving forward, having important goals are not achieved overnight, they necessitate, and no they demand patience, perseverance, and persistence. If you persistently take action, you will build momentum. "If Columbus had ever thought to turn back, no one would have blamed him. No one would have memorized him either."

In the face of challenge, perseverance ensures that we continue to take action towards the accomplishment of our objective. As World's famous educationalist points out, this may require us to frequent adjustments to our tactics, until we achieve the objective.

"If you have an important point to make, don't try to be subtle or clever. Use a pile driver. Hit the point once. Then come back and hit it again. Then hit it a third time - a tremendous whack."—Winston S. Churchill

Reflecting on your objectives…

• Do you require amending the strategies you are using to archive your goal?

• Have you persevered toward your objective? Or have you perhaps given up too soon?

There are two mentalities: buckle down and achieve your objectives, or not bother since you likely won't succeed in any case. In spite of the fact that this may appear to be an oversimplification, we think this oblivious choice has an aggravating impact all through your life. In the event that you are in the camp of "making a decent attempt leads to achievement", you invest more energy, you take rejection in your stride (despite the fact that regardless it harms), you get up every single time you fall, and you feel motivated to attempt and attempt and try again until you succeed. Whether it's a spelling bee or beginning your own organization: trusting you can accomplish something through diligent work is a critical element for success. Be in the other camp of "you won't succeed" paying little heed to what you do, there is an unequivocally negative example. You feel that whatever you do throughout everyday life, you presumably won't succeed in any case, so you don't feel inspired to attempt in any case. When you confront difficulties and hurdles, you see that as a sign that you will fail. When you are rejected, again you feel weak, powerless and unfortunate.

In psychology, there's an idea called "locus of control": an individual's conviction about how long they can control the events around them: do you take control of the things you can control, or do you blame external components for your prosperity or disappointment. Sooner or later the vast majority have most likely identified with both camps. However, we imagine that over the time goes there is a huge exacerbating impact, encountering little hurdles and difficulties and after that success, which inspires you to handle bigger challenges and to feel well prepared for greater misfortunes.

Set your psyche to an objective, something that you believe is bizarre and afterward buckles down to accomplish it. Depending upon the "challenge" you pick – it might take the number of hours or only a week. Learn a language, run more distant than you might suspect you could, and figure out how to cook another dish, get the courage to complete an open talking in Public, climb a mountain, build something, influence something, and create something. Set an objective that scares you a little and drives you out of your comfort zone. The truth is that you have accomplished something that you thought was unimaginable and not possible, you will be raring to go for your next toughest challenge and more resilient to the hindrances that you will unavoidably face out and along the way.

Here are 4 reasons Perseverance is vital to your prosperity and success:

## 1. PERSEVERANCE HELPS YOU CONQUER THE UNEXPECTED

At the point when things don't work out as

expected, it's tempting to surrender. We lose our confidence and consider moving onward to something that is less demanding. This is actually what the vast majorities of people do on the grounds that we're anxious about disappointment or failure and evade far from things that are hard and necessary. Plans make us feel safe, yet be prepared when things turn out of your control so you can land on your feet. You may need to change course and adjust somehow. Your objective continues to be the same as before, however, your roadmap may need to be changed. Try to develop a nimble mentality by attempting to anticipate potential misfortunes and have an alternate course of action for them.

## 2. PERSEVERANCE ENABLES YOU TO KEEP FOCUSED

At the point when things turn out badly, it is difficult to keep up motivation and core interest. Perseverance enables you to stay concentrated on long haul objectives so you can change your behavior accordingly. Regularly, this expects you to hold feelings in line to keep emotions in check from sabotaging your endeavors and efforts to continue advancing and moving forward. Visualize yourself achieving your objective regardless of what it takes. Watch out for the objective and see yourself reaching the end.

## 3.    PERSEVERANCE    IS    FED    BY ENCOURAGEMENT AND SUPPORT

At the point when things turn out of your control, discover support and cncouragement from people around you whom you trust and respect. In view of their experience and ability, search out their recommendation, suggestions, and proposals on the how to proficiently continue moving ahead. Successful individuals with perseverance comprehend that still need to do the tough work, yet it is extremely encouraging when you are surrounded with positive back up. We in our own island as a whole need other individuals' assistance and support. It may be a short talk or a couple of words of assistance. Be the individual who connects when you require assistance rather than to surrender. Do not be afraid to share your situations with other people, however, be particular about it. Ensure they are individuals who really need what is best for you and will give you both valuable and positive feedback. Seek for "mirror" companions or friends who will be fair, cherishing, honest, and objective.

## 4. PERSEVERANCE MAKES YOU DIG DEEP DOWN

If you are on a path that has meaning, value, and significance for you, you are unquestionably on the right path, so keep going. If you are not, then a delay or failure will be enough to make you surrender and try something else. Success can be exceptionally misleading on the grounds that frequently it is the place we remain, regardless of whether it's what truly fills us or not. It is a success that is based in complacency because we are too scared of failure to pursue the type of work that would offer worth and meaning. Don't take the easiest path, dig deep down where it counts and discovers the things that you can't leave. When you are pursuing that sort of objective, it won't make any difference what other individuals say on the grounds that your inner vision is far stronger than any external hindrance you will come up against.

Taking everything into account, in short,

persistence is an essential piece of life. Its isolates the complete from the incomplete and just to recap, here are the 5 key reasons why having perseverance satisfies:

• Most successful persons have failed in any event once

• People jump at the chance to test you on the determination

• What comes effectively typically isn't justified, despite any potential benefits

• Knowledge isn't picked up without ingenuity and persistence

• The more you accomplish something, the better you get at it

Permanence, perseverance, and persistence in spite of all obstacles, discouragements, and impossibilities: It is this that in all things distinguishes the strong soul from the weak.

Our mind is incredibly powerful (lot more than you imagine) and with a bit of guidance and mind training, you can completely change your frame of mind. What this actually states is that you can pin down all those magical moments that you have stopped noticing while you hunt after the clock, which, unlike you, by no means has to make any stops. Just try to believe in yourself. You cannot uncover beauty outside if you cannot see it inside yourself. If you are always seeking outward approval you are seriously going to lose precious time. And that is the time you could have spent dreaming about your upcoming big projector or developing any new skill you want to be trained. When you start believing in your abilities and yourself, the possibilities become never-ending. You turn into an imaginative and inspired human being, you dare to grow, you dare to dream, you dare to share your dreams with other people, and you lose your terror of being ridiculed for it. Planning. Education. Desire. All these start contributing to your success part but none of them are sufficient without persistence. – Michael Josephson. Everything starts with a vision, an idea, or yes a dream. The dissimilarity between people who believe in themselves & people who do not is that the people who do believe they will be able to take one step ahead than their strength permits them. And that's when the miracles come into view and they end up triumph no one thought they ever could. "Magic believes in yourself, if you can do that, you can make anything happen." -Johann Wolfgang von Goethe- So, try to get yourself moving. We're all the makers of our own lives. We can act in a lot of dissimilar ways and influence the situations we find ourselves in, and how we take action in all these times will lead to a convincing result.

So it's significant to know what mental state you are in when you are about to take steps. If you are acting from a place of love, understanding, care and, compassion, your actions will surely be graceful, magical, and influential and they will also be part of a better life. When you act out of love you won't very soon feel better, however, you will also inspire other people to do it too. Love always attracts extra love, and that goes way beyond the real results of any action on its own. But if your trials of actions come from your ego, if they have a basis in mistrust, criticism, terror, or suspicion, you'll just attract those similar things. You'll attract a similar type of situations and people over & over again. Now it is the time to change that. Don't be frightened. There is magic waiting for you around the corner, and the finest part is that you can create it. Actually, we have already gone into so many ingredients to create magic, now it's in our hands to magnetize it.

Here are some of the significant things that helped you keep going that day and bring the magic of persistence in your life when everything in you wanted to quit. If you find yourself in circumstances where you want to stop or give up, these lessons can help you, too.

1. Ignore others- At the beginning of the mountaineering, you can only see the people passing in front of you. Every time you see someone hiking without extra effort, you might feel bad about yourself. But when you stopped comparing and stopped worrying everyone else's journey to your own, you seriously began to concentrate on your own mission and how you are going to attain it. As you work toward your vision, it can be simple to get distracted when you see others attaining their objectives faster, easier, far better than you. It can make you feel unsatisfied

and disappointed with your own progress. But when it comes to vectoring a goal, what's happening with others is extraneous when it detracts from your capability to move forward. When tackling a hard task, you need each ounce of energy you can muster. Just ensure to channel it to the right place that will propel you forward.

2. Become your own biggest follower- When you start climbing, you weren't alone. But within 10 minutes, you could be behind and alone. At first, you might be frustrated your companions abandoned you in your time of need. But then you could realize your burden was not theirs to bear. Even though it can be energizing to have others around to encourage and assist you, having them there is a luxury, not a necessity. That lesson allowed you to turn inward and find in yourself the strength, persistence, and willpower to keep going. You began to encourage and high-five yourself with every single step. Sometimes on the path to victory, you have to walk alone. If you find yourself in that similar position, just find a way to give yourself what you need to carry on.

3. Try to appreciate the small things- You began

the trek before the sun was up. As you continued to mount, it started to peek around the mountain, giving glimpses of the sparkling beauty all around you. It could be miraculous. During the catch-your-breath breaks, you marveled at the privilege of seeing the natural world in all her beauty. In those moments, you gave no thought to your struggle. You could be too busy being gratifying for being right there. It can be simple to focus all your energy on reaching your ultimate objective. But if the only thing you can see is your end purpose, you will miss the beauty of the trip along the way. The new experiences and welcome surprises give you much-required fuel to keep going.

4. Focus on the next step- It can discourage you to think how far away you are from the top. So you might reframe your vision into mini-milestones that made the next steps more manageable. Simply take one more step, you thought. OK, now simply get over to those tough stones. And yes once you get to that the track you can stop and rest for a few minutes. When your objectives seem too big, it can feel impossible, which opens the path for

resistance to creep in. By breaking your goal into bite-sized pieces, you can keep yourself in motion, persistence and build momentum.

5. Lastly, you can try avoiding your watch- Before the trek; you read that there are so many people make it to the top of the mountain in about 45-60 minutes. But it took you so long. When you focused on the time it was supposed to take, you might get frustrated at yourself for not being fast or good enough. But no one cared how long it took me to hike and get to the top and you should not have, either. All that mattered was finishing your journey. As you work on accomplishing your goals, stop looking at the clock. Stop calculating yourself against something or somebody else. It will only serve to distract you from concentrating on what you require to do right now to advance.

6. Stop looking for a way out- Not everybody who goes to mountaineering or hikes. You can easily take a bus straight to the top & save yourself the physical and emotional tension. Early on in your climb, you might think about retreating or waving down the bus on their way up. When your pain is at the forefront, it is normal to want to make it go

away. However, when you spend time seeking a way to abort your journey, you waste valuable energy that could be used to help you conquer momentary pain and distress for long-term growth.

7. Acknowledge your limitations- You had to be honest with yourself. You were having difficulty getting air and you could not keep the pace of the group. Simply, pushing your body to the limit by trying to keep a speedy pace was not going to work for you. Your path needed to be diverse, and that's OK. After implementing your new tactic, the journey was less exhausting. Your path to success might not look like everybody else's. That's OK. Everybody's situation is poles apart. Instead, acknowledge where you are, so you can offer yourself what you require to be thriving. As you work to attain your objectives, there will be obstructions, bumps, blockages, and bruises along the way. When the journey becomes more painful than what you are used to, it can be simple to throw in the towel & retreat. However, if you follow these lessons, you can find the power to keep going in the midst of complexity. And when you persevere, you will discover the reward was

worth the effort. Just so not give up.

As you grow old, you realize that there are real-life strengths that push you to be successful in life and your preferred career and profession.

Our mindset is incredibly influential (lot more than you imagine) and with a bit of guidance and mind training, you can completely change your frame of mind. What this actually states is that you can pin down all those magical moments that you have stopped noticing while you hunt after the clock, which, unlike you, by no means has to make any stops. Just try to believe in yourself. You cannot uncover beauty outside if you cannot see it inside yourself. If you are always seeking outward approval you are seriously going to lose precious time. And that is the time you could have spent dreaming about your upcoming big projector or developing any new skill you want to be trained. When you start believing in your abilities and yourself, the possibilities become never-ending. You turn into an imaginative and inspired human being, you dare to grow, you dare to dream, you dare to share your dreams with other people, and you lose your terror of being ridiculed for it. Plan and desire start contributing to your success part but none of them are sufficient without persistence. – Michael Josephson. Everything starts with a vision, an idea, or yes a dream. The dissimilarity between people who believe in themselves & people who do not is that the people who do believe they will be able to take one step ahead than their strength permits them. And that's when the miracles come into view and they end up triumph no one thought they ever could. "Magic believes in yourself, if you can do that, you can make anything happen." -Johann Wolfgang von Goethe- So, try to get yourself moving. We're all the makers of our own lives. We can act in a lot of dissimilar ways and influence the situations we find ourselves in, and how we take action in all these times will lead to a convincing result.

So it's significant to know what mental state you are in when you are about to take steps. If you are acting from a place of love, understanding, care and, compassion, your actions will surely be graceful, magical, and influential and they will also be part of a better life. When you act out of love you won't very soon feel better, however, you will also inspire other people to do it too. Love and affection always draw towards extra affection, and that goes way beyond the real results of any act on its own. But if your trials of actions come from your ego, if they have a basis in mistrust, criticism, terror, or suspicion, you'll just attract those similar things. You'll attract a similar type of situations and people over & over again. Now it is the time to change that. Don't be frightened. There is magic waiting for you around the corner, and the finest part is that you can create it. Actually, we have already gone into so many ingredients to create magic, now it's in our hands to magnetize it.

Here are some of the significant things that helped you keep going that day and bring the magic of persistence in your life when everything in you wanted to quit. If you find yourself in circumstances where you want to stop or give up, these lessons can help you, too.

1. Ignore others- At the beginning of the mountaineering, you can only see the people passing in front of you. Every time you see someone hiking without extra effort, you might feel bad about yourself. But when you stopped

comparing and stopped worrying everyone else's journey to your own, you seriously began to concentrate on your own mission and how you are going to attain it. As you work toward your vision, it can be simple to get distracted when you see others attaining their objectives faster, easier, far better than you. It can make you feel unsatisfied and disappointed with your own progress. But when it comes to vectoring a goal, what's happening with others is extraneous when it detracts from your capability to move forward. When tackling a hard task, you need each ounce of energy you can muster. Just ensure to channel it to the right place that will propel you forward.

2. Become your own biggest follower- When you start climbing, you weren't alone. But within 10 minutes, you could be behind and alone. At first, you might be frustrated your companions abandoned you in your time of need. But then you could realize your burden was not theirs to bear. Even though it can be energizing to have others around to encourage and assist you, having them there is a luxury, not a necessity. That lesson allowed you to turn inward and find in yourself the

strength, persistence, and willpower to keep going. You began to encourage and high-five yourself with every single step. Sometimes on the path to victory, you have to walk alone. If you find yourself in that similar position, just find a way to give yourself what you need to carry on.

3. Try to appreciate the small things- You began the trek before the sun was up. As you continued to mount, it started to peek around the mountain, giving glimpses of the sparkling beauty all around you. It could be miraculous. During the catch-your-breath breaks, you marveled at the privilege of seeing the natural world in all her beauty. In those moments, you gave no thought to your struggle. You could be too busy being gratifying for being right there. It can be simple to focus all your energy on reaching your ultimate objective. But if the only thing you can see is your end purpose, you will miss the beauty of the trip along the way. The new experiences and welcome surprises give you much-required fuel to keep going.

4. Focus on the next step- It can discourage you to think how far away you are from the top. So you

might reframe your vision into mini-milestones that made the next steps more manageable. Simply take one more step, you thought. OK, now simply get over to those tough stones. And yes once you get to that the track you can stop and rest for a few minutes. When your objectives seem too big, it can feel impossible, which opens the path for resistance to creep in. By breaking your goal into bite-sized pieces, you can keep yourself in motion, persistence and build momentum.

5. Lastly, you can try avoiding your watch- Before the trek; you read that there are so many people make it to the top of the mountain in about 45-60 minutes. But it took you so long. When you focused on the time it was supposed to take, you might get frustrated at yourself for not being fast or good enough. But no one cared how long it took me to hike and get to the top and you should not have, either. All that mattered was finishing your journey. As you work on accomplishing your goals, stop looking at the clock. Stop calculating yourself against something or somebody else. It will only serve to distract you from concentrating on what you require to do right now to advance.

6. Stop looking for a way out- Not everybody who goes to mountaineering or hikes. You can easily take a bus straight to the top & save yourself the physical and emotional tension. Early on in your climb, you might think about retreating or waving down the bus on their way up. When your pain is at the forefront, it is normal to want to make it go away. However, when you spend time seeking a way to abort your journey, you waste valuable energy that could be used to help you conquer momentary pain and distress for long-term growth.

7. Acknowledge your limitations- You had to be honest with yourself. You were having difficulty getting air and you could not keep the pace of the group. Simply, pushing your body to the limit by trying to keep a speedy pace was not going to work for you. Your path needed to be diverse, and that's OK. After implementing your new tactic, the journey was less exhausting. Your path to success might not look like everybody else's. That's OK. Everybody's situation is poles apart. Instead, acknowledge where you are, so you can offer yourself what you require to be thriving. As you work to attain your objectives, there will be

obstructions, bumps, blockages, and bruises along the way. When the journey becomes more painful than what you are used to, it can be simple to throw in the towel & retreat. However, if you follow these lessons, you can find the power to keep going in the midst of complexity. And when you persevere, you will discover the reward was worth the effort. Just so not give up.

As you grow old, you realize that there are real-life strengths that push you to be successful in life and your preferred career and profession.

- Creativity
- Charisma
- Physical abilities
- Cognitive control
- Artistic talent
- And even charisma

So, the harsh truth that most of us countenance at some point in our lives is that we are not the strongest, prettiest, smartest, fastest, or most talented person in the room. Does that mean you are doomed and will never outrageously succeed in your career? No, not at all. It does mean that you need the perfect plan and strategy that doesn't depend on innate talent to carry the day.

There is hope- Some of you know that you are remarkably talented, gorgeous, superstars, super genius. If so, you do not need any advice and you do not need anybody's help. You are already ruling the earth. Go in peace, follow the magic of persistence my friends. Now, for those who are still in search and want to know the secret, rest assured: there is hope for the rest of your life. Perhaps there are few among us who will admit that they are in this group of hope conception. You may not always be the most talented, smartest, and most imaginative person in the room. However, you can tap into these three superpowers and still attain great success in your life, love, and career.

You simply need to be:

- Consistent
- Resistant
- Persistent

You just do not mean to have persistent, resistant, and consistent traits. You also need to exhibit heroic levels of each. But, the great news is that anybody can do this if they are truly ambitious, dedicated, willing, and as stubborn as famous personalities like Steve Jobs.

- **Consistent**

You create new habits easily and you are consistent with those habits. James Clear has an excellent story on this. Process beats goal sets. Systems will hit vision. Try to concentrate more on what you will consistently do each day and you will achieve more than dreaming about what you want. As people fall in love with planning and goals, and then they get discouraged when things went wrong (as they always do in the end). Or, they want the outcomes, but they really do not want to constantly put in the hard work required. Fall in love with the everyday procedure and enjoy the journey. The outcomes are a side effect. They are nice, of course. It is fun to celebrate the victories along the way. The truth is when you truly start loving the process you will tolerate the hard times and setbacks. The failure here or there does not destroy you. You become overcharged and persistence work as bulletproof. Keep on, move on and you cannot help but see great results. "We are what we repeatedly do. Excellence, then, is not an act, but a habit." —Aristotle

### • **Resistant**

Resistance is the right word for "extremely stubborn." If somebody tells you that you cannot do anything, you should prove them wrong by doing it. Maybe you will even do it twice (like mundane events). If somebody tells you that you must do something, it fuels your willpower and drives to never do that thing. But, more often than not, it may push you or enable you to accomplish things that shouldn't have been possible for someone like you. Or, at least that is what you were told. I was told that I was too poor to go to college.

How many times has someone told you that you weren't good enough to do something? It wasn't because they are willing to spend their lives that way. Just follow the magic of persistence and resist anyone who tells you what you can and can't do with your life. They do not have an idea or know the drive or fire that you have inside. They do not completely understand what you are capable of doing if you persevere. They don't have to live your life. Only you have to. So, "Don't let others define you. You define yourself."—Ginni Rometty

- **Persistent**

"We don't get a chance to do that many things, and everyone should be really excellent. Because this is our life"—*Steve Jobs.* When you are trying to solve a problem or learn something new, you should refuse to give up. You get tunnel vision and you can persist until you get it done, one way or the different ways. Daniel Goleman would call this "Grit" and he considered that it is the biggest predictors of your success. It does not for all time mean that the solution needs to come from me. Sometimes it means that you hire or take assistance from someone who can provide you the solution. But, you should persist until it is done. Just be stubborn, try the magical persistence and refuse to give up or be stopped. This is a magical superpower that only a few have. But now you can easily try and can do this! Anybody can be persistent, set their sights on something, and keep grinding to make it happen. You do not fully agree with every aspect of but, you can believe in the philosophy of persistence.

"Nothing in this world can take the place of persistence. Talent will not: nothing is more common than unsuccessful men with talent. Genius will not; unrewarded genius is almost a proverb. Education will not: the world is full of educated derelicts. Persistence and determination alone are omnipotent."— Calvin Coolidge

You might have a boatload of knowledge, talent, skills, and experience. Everybody does, in their own approach. But, don't worry if you are not the absolute best at everything. Be consistent, persistent, and resistant. Those superpowers are accessible to all of us. Inherent talent can only take you so far. However, the big three will take you the rest of the way. *Permanence, perseverance, and persistence in spite of all obstacles, discouragements and impossibilities: It is this that in all things distinguishes the strong soul from the weak.-Thomas Carlyle*

Persistence is where you get mental strength. Perseverance and determination will carve you as a leader in your industry. It makes you extraordinary and separates you from normal people. You must learn to cultivate a habit of persistence since everything is possible if you persevere. The persistent man or woman does not accept defeat, he just keeps climbing on it. It has incredible magic and power. To reach the zenith tower, if we took one step at a time and continue to take slow and steady steps and not stop. People of greatness have finished the race for success while encountering all the hurdles that are hurled their way, which generally deters common people. Perseverance is a crucial step on your path, to reach your dream. People, in order to live to his fullest potential, must have a vision. To reach that goal you must build your own route. The first step is willpower and the second is dedication, the third is the positive attitude and the fourth is discipline, and the final step is the most imperative being persistent. "Some people have greatness thrust upon them. Very few have excellence thrust upon them." --John W. Gardner

The individual with determination and persistence will succeed over the person with extra talent, more money or higher education. Nothing can replace perseverance not talent nor education, neither genius. Lack of persistence is a weak spot which filters all the way through a majority of the races. Persistence can turn hardship into greatness. Read Autobiographies and Biographies of famous personalities. Follow some of the principles they had engaged to succeed. You can make the right choice today. Focus on the kind of result you want to produce. Set the target for this year. Set tools to work with, to attain this target. Fall in love with your dream and discipline your life. Remember all great people started as average human beings but had a passion, dream, persisted, endured, strong-minded, disciplined, devoted and with a positive mental attitude attained their goals. If they can persist, so you can, so embark on to persist.

*Winston Saga is one of the world's leading sales legends. He is also the CEO of Sales and Motivation International. Winston has been acknowledged as a unique and distinctive authority in the field of sales and personal development. Last year International Biography Centre selected him "International Man of the Year" for his outstanding contribution to sales and Service. He has written 100's of articles to magazine, journals and websites. If you're going through hell, keep going. — Winston Churchill*

If you are seriously going to attain excellence in big things, you develop the habit in little matters. Brilliance is not an exception; it is a prevailing approach and attitude.

## The Power of Persistence

Just believe in yourself even others do not. If you

are not at the level you need to be, discover a means to make yourself better. "I've failed over and over and over again in my life. And that is why I succeed." -- Michael Jordan. Ever one craves success. But simply waiting for it, however, would not guarantee success and achievement. That is the key reasons why there are so many people fail to attain their goal: They encounter adversity, suffering, and give up. So let's discuss one characteristic required to achieve what you set out to do: Persistence is the blend of powerful desire and determination. Once upon a time, a person named Paul encountered tremendous obstacles like physical punishment, shipwreck, constant danger, etc., but he chooses never to quit. What motivated Paul to persist amidst struggles? He had a clear goal and trusted that his strong willpower would enable him to achieve it. Paul had his eyes fixed on his ultimate purpose, which he so valued that no situation could deter him. At the end of the day, he achieved what had ordained. Just like the Father have great goals for his kids. Striving for anything less will neither accomplish his nor achieve what he has intended in his life.

Once your direction is obvious and clear, you should passionately pursue those goals with the strength and proper guidance—especially when hardship and obstacles arise.

Do not give up! It's how you rise from a collapse that truly defines you as a strong person. For instance the Basketball legend Michael Jordan knows a lot about perseverance and determination. Discussing his stellar career he once illustrated that he had lost almost 300 games and had even missed more than 9 thousand shots. On 26 occasions when he had been hand over with the game-winning shot he had flunked, stated Michael Jordan, "I've failed over and over and over again in my life and that's why I succeed." Eventually, the fact is he succeeded because he persevered. He persisted. He wasn't ready to be a quitter. So, no matter how many times he was fouled (and he was considered one of the most fouled players in the sport's history) he got up and kept going. We can all learn from him and his never quitting perception. Persistence truly pays and makes a way out. One historical classic example you have almost certainly heard and encounter before is that of famous personality-Thomas Edison who said that when developing the electric light bulb he hadn't quit and failed—he had just found 10,000 ways that did not work. Thomas Edison was a veritable and most admired quote machine on the subject of persistence. He also said, "Many of life's failures are people who did not realize how close they were to success when they gave up." And, "Genius is one percent inspiration, 99% perspiration." Persistence. Perspiration. Dogged determination. These are important traits that go a long way in the business world. The majority of the entrepreneurs in their journey to ultimate success occasionally stumbles and now and then takes serious falls. But, like Edison and Jordan, they keep on going for the reason that they know that they have to endure rejection and failure if they want to become the finest in their respective fields of endeavor. If they want to come out on zenith level.

Since the earliest days of his career when he started his passion for the game, he might have encountered obstacles large and small. He overcame them all and continues to do so because of the power of persistence in him, which gave him more confidence, personality, passion, and conviction so that he never give up. Often the only obvious difference between losers and winners is persistence. Losers fold their cards when hardship enters their lives. However, winners never ever give up. Believe in yourself and be prepared to get your skates on. According to research around 75-80 % of all sales, for instance, take place between the fifth and twelfth probability of contact. Just think about that. Just think, how many people are willing to ask for the sale fifth, six, seven, eight times or else more? Majority of them give up by that stage. You have to bear in your mind—whether you are trying to make a sale, plan a trip, prepare for the competitive exams, or achieve anything else in life's great journey—that every time someone says "no" it is just one step closer to somebody saying "yes."

Can anyone develop the power of persistence? Of course, they can. It's one of those great abilities that lie inside all of us. You have a mindset and brain to use. You just have to be confident and to take a leap of faith. You simply have to put them into action. It doesn't matter how capable you are, it is not going to get you anywhere in life without perseverance and willpower. Being determined also means being able to develop a thick skin and handle things when it doesn't go your way. Being able to "stick with it" and keep on moving in your journey with the confidence that when one dream ends a shining new dream is just beginning. It is the magic of the cosmos. Being persistent critically means to overcome any fears that might be holding you back. Fear of making blunders, fear of failure, fear of breakdown, and as well as fear of rejection. Make the bold and strong decision to doggedly pursue your goals. It is the only means you will reach your final destination. Being persistent and determined logically means being willing to do extra and do it more often than the average person would. You go to one more meeting. You can make extra efforts. You make that one last business deals or sales call just before finishing for the day. Conduct more research than your colleagues. Take a course that will advance your career. Push yourself to learn something new. Successful people persist in going the extra mile. They never stop dreaming about the next attempt that will take them to the stars. So, being persistent means being relentless. Never give up. Never surrender. The power of persistence will get you the ultimate prize while others fall by the wayside. As a wise person once said, "You may be dissatisfied if you fail, but you are more destined if you never try at all."

Being persistent and determined is the one thing which isolates the champs from the failures. At the point when an individual makes up his or her mind to achieve a specific accomplishment and set their focus toward that path, declining to be stopped, he or she normally gets what they followed. The intensity of persistence, even notwithstanding difficulty, is the true traits of champions. For sure, the individuals who accomplish incredible things are the individuals who don't realize when to stop. From others, they hear insulting comments and critics continually remind them, over again and again, that what they are endeavoring to do, won't work. However, they continue to persevere.

Advice from good-natured companions and alliances to take their misfortunes like a man or lady does not dissuade the true winner in life. Stopping isn't in the vocabulary of success and powerful individuals. Finding another approach to achieve objectives is fine. Searching for alternate paths to a similar destiny is okay. In any case, to the challenge and courage of heart, there is no such reality as stopping. Being relentless is the one thing which isolates the victors from the losers. At the point when an individual makes up his or her mind to achieve a specific feat and set their concentration toward that path, declining to be deterred, he or she typically gets what they followed.

The principle is simple but significant. It has made winners out of many and keeps on doing as such. Apply this principle and you will taste the sweetness of triumph. Live by this principle and you will experience accomplishment again and again. Instruct this experience with other people and you will experience success over and over again. Being in presence works in this principle to perfection. This principle is in pretty much every achievement book ever written. A portion of those who lived by this principle saw its astonishing outcomes, determined to share what they learned, through their compositions. Unfortunately, numerous individuals don't invest in their books to take in a win rule or success principle that is old, but then new, for each time an individual activates the principle, the outcome in that individual's life is new, sweet, and ground-breaking. The principle is simple: know what you need, you will have what you need, and seek after it persistently, until the point when you get it.

Would it be able to be that simple, some may inquire? Is that really the way to progress? The response is a resounding YES. We challenge you to read after those who have accomplished an extraordinary proportion of achievement and check whether they didn't apply this principle. It will be proven genuine that if you are persistent in a good thing, and you decline to stop, sooner or later, what you seek after will find you. "Nothing on the planet can replace Persistence. Talent won't; nothing is more common than unsuccessful men with talent and ability. Genius won't; unrewarded Genius is just like a proverb. Education won't; the world is loaded with educated derelicts. Constancy and Persistence alone are omnipotent. The motto 'Go ahead' has solved and will take carc of the issues of the human race." The conventional definition of persistence is: "Declining to surrender or given up; persevering resolutely; firm or unshakable continuance in n a course of action despite trouble or resistance." Is anyone wonder then, that perseverance is the fundamental principal distinction between a successful result and a failed outcome? In that case, it behooves us to build up the essential traits of determination and perseverance.

If you're going through hell, keep going. -- Winston Churchill. What about Colonel Sanders, the founder of Kentucky Fried Chicken? He was a military retiree and had nothing to his name, aside from his mom's chicken recipe formula. So what did he do? He took his old sports wagon out and started driving to many restaurants after restaurant after restaurant. His purpose was to offer the Chicken recipe formula, yet he was turned down consistently, multiple times 1,007 times before he received his first yes. That one yes is the thing that made Kentucky Fried Chicken possible. We keep going with story after story of those who had to be adaptable, imaginative, flexible, and above all persistent regardless of failing hundreds, sometimes a large number of times. You can also learn from Steve Jobs. He's had had movies made about his story, so you are likely more comfortable with the difficulties and challenges he faced in becoming one of the success and wealthiest corporations on the planet. Members of his own board of directors betrayed him out of his own business. He could have enabled this to stop him; but instead, he chooses to come back to Apple and voted back in as the Apple's Chairman. He created the iPhone, the iPod, and the fresh line of Mac Laptops. Businesses today are incomprehensible without your iPhone.

The three great essentials to achieve anything worthwhile are, first, hard work; second, stick-to-itiveness; third, common sense." -- Thomas A. Edison

A standout and the most essential qualities for all of us to develop is the ability to persevere through life's difficulties and obstacles. It is very significant to constantly be aware of that EVERYTHING COUNTS throughout our life. Every single action you take daily either rewards you somehow or harms you. Everything either takes away or adds up. Everything either adds to your prosperity or moves you far from it. Nothing you do is unbiased. And all achievement is, at last, the triumph of perseverance. The Power of Persistence helping you to skips once more from difficulties and inspires you to become unstoppable toward accomplishing your objectives.

Stage 1 to getting into the magic of Persistence is to know where you are today and in addition know where you need to go. At the end of the day, shooting darts in the dark and seeking for the best is equal to living your life without clear objectives. Try not to stress if your objective seems unrealistic. Before the Wright Brothers, it was out of mind to feel that a man could fly in a plane. What's more, before yesterday December 8, 2007, a sophomore has never won a Heisman Trophy. It's safe to say that if you can vision it; want it bad enough; and willing to sacrifice and persist, almost anything is achievable. Step 2 is to make peace and harmony with the fact that you will face one obstruction after another to achieve your objective. Some goals are short-term and can be accomplished in a while or in a year. Other objectives might take a lifetime to accomplish. In either case, you will continue to face hurdles and you need to prepare yourself to meet them head-on with self-belief. You need to ACCEPT that they'll be there. How could it be another way? No person is all-knowing, so misfortunes and setbacks are BUILT INTO our life's path.

Stage 3 is to persevere and defeat every obstruction en route UNTIL you achieve your objective. The energy and drive to persevere under the harsh situations is the thing that separates the individuals who make it to the end goal. At the point when obstacles show up...you must PERSIST. When you don't know which approach to turn...get help and PERSIST. And most importantly, if you ever think that you're defeated find an approach to continue onward and PERSIST. Furthermore, Help and assistance for the most persistent people wonderfully seem to appear from some of the most unexpected individuals and places at the opportune time. Persevering people simply appear to figure out how to step forward and prop up when circumstances become difficult. The history books are loaded with these motivating stories.

Obstructions are tough. They knock you down. But they are not intended to KEEP you down. They are intended to revitalize your will, your boldness, your confidence, and your energy. Anyone can succeed and do well staying strong with the breeze at their backs. But what about when the when the wind is at your face and you end up ON your back? As Tiger Woods said in regards to the terrible days, "you have to find it within yourself to get it done." Researchers have discovered that individuals that define obvious objectives for themselves, and decline to stop, will bounce back from any from any misfortunes and accomplish MOST of their objectives. At the end of the day, you can accomplish any objective you set for yourself as long as you fight till your last trail, and decline to allow the inevitable difficulties and frustrations to dissuade you from your course.

**Find the Power of Persistence**

**Here are suggestions for achievement in any field, and some other objective you strive for everyday life:**

- Be determined.
- Be stubborn!
- Do not take no for an answer.
- Be single-minded.
- Learn from your mistakes—widen your horizons.
- Don't limit yourself. You may need to take

a major move to get the start you need.

- Seek out every single chance.

- Read as much as possible.

- Never think you aren't good enough.

- Develop a set of connections and leverage it.

- Seek out new experiences and environments, and chiefly anyone with a wealth of experience.

- Collect a few qualifications (a degree, maybe an industry certificate) but then make it a priority to collect contacts and experiences, too.

Take time right now to assess your own circumstances and determine your next point of convergence for increasing your persistence in financial matters. Whatever your big, recent accomplishment, select a new one slightly larger and requiring a longer time commitment. Then lay out your plan and get started. Plan now to keep repeating this process, congratulating yourself occasionally for your growing ability for persistent work, until consistent work on all your goals is naturally kept up with ease. In this way, you will experience the power of persistence for yourself.

## ABOUT THE AUTHOR

Positive Thinking Mentor Author Gautam Sharma(gautamsharma.contact@gmail.com)-an intelligent, accomplished, capable, creative professional was born in India, has lived in Asia, Europe, Africa and now living in USA embodies and edifies positive thinking, power of optimism and is sharing insights into human behavior and human potential through philosophical, psychological perspectives with the view of sharing mankind's centuries-old wisdom plus proven, research findings so as to empower people worldwide. The author plans to utilize his strengths of professionalism, wide, varied experiences, creativity and communications' skills to publish the Empowerment Series on improvement, self-help topics. Thank you valued readers for your continuous support, contributions and your favorable feedback. Wishing everybody abundance of positive thinking and better living through the power of optimism.

OTHER BOOKS BY THE AUTHOR

https://www.amazon.com/POSITIVE-THINKING-OPTIMISM-Original-English-ebook/dp/B01HRY684S/ref=asap_bc?ie=UTF8

also

https://www.amazon.com/SELF-CONFIDENCE-ESTEEM-HAPPINESS-SUCCESS-ebook/dp/B076VM1MNR/ref=tmm_kin_swatch_0?_encoding=UTF8&qid=&sr=

and

https://www.amazon.com/JOY-forHEALTHY-HAPPY-LIVING-Empowerment-ebook/dp/B078L6Y1YM/ref=sr_1_5?s=digital-text&ie=UTF8&qid=1515281796&sr=1-5

Discover your full potential: The Universe within

Gautam Sharma

(Dedicated to valued readers, especially those who write positive reviews)


KEEP GOING TO SUCCEED     ALWAYS

# PERSISTENCE BEATS INTELLIGENCE FOR SUCCESS

**Gautam Sharma**

**and**

**1.**

**SHORMISTHA CHATTERJEE**

**1.**

**( Dedicated to valued readers)**

# COPYRIGHT

## Table of Contents

INTRODUCTION Would you like to get what you want in life every time? Become more a happy long term, be more youthful with healthy body, keep joyous relationships, have satisfying work and income, enjoy big houses, cars, and vacations? Ever wondered how so many people are successful and some lead extraordinary lives-s far as changing countries and causes? Think for a moment about the greatest people over history. There is a distinct, common attribute that has made many men and women extremely successful and renowned over centuries and across continents. From Alexander the Great( 356 BC ) to Cleopatra, Genghis Khan, Michael Angelo, Joan of Arc, Mahatma Gandhi, Winston Churchill, Marie Curie, Einstein, Thomas Edison, Benjamin Franklin to present day outstanding people as Bill Gates, Warren Buffet, some other billionaires and world leaders. It's just not mental or physical prowess, talents, education, training or good luck that worked for them. The outstanding common attribute among all successful and extraordinary people of excellence across all space and time has been the quality of persistence, attitude, and motivation.

It's been about keeping on going towards their goals in the face of denials, obstacles, failures, and opposition. The unstoppable keep on going; whatever the odds, slowdowns or roadblocks and they achieve success, victory, and fame. This book will help you gain the magic of persistence, motivation and determined attitude. You can also become very persistent and super successful. Let us look at what it is and why it is so important. Persistence is the attitude and the personality trait to continue with determination on a set course of action to overcome difficulties, failures or opposition until the required goals are achieved. There are several reasons why persistence is important:

1. 1. It shows that you are ambitious and that you have high goals and objectives to

achieve. If you want to go to some places, you will have reason to find ways to reach there.

2. 2. Your ambition and subsequent drive make you stand out and make others notice your determined, dominant personality.

3. 3. Persistence makes you garner skills, experiences, and abilities. The process of working harder to overcome failure helps you acquire new, peripheral skills or hone onto the current ones.

4. Working harder helps build inner strength and stamina. The determination to think and work is to keep going on doing activities methodically and consistently going step by step doing activities that are required for your goals. Reasons Why Persistence is the Key to Success?

In simple words, persistence means the attitude and personality trait of working hard and trying again and again until complete success is achieved. Here is why persistence is the key to success and why you should develop it as a vital personality trait.

1. Persistence makes you an expert

You may not be good at doing something for the first time but you will get better at it when you keep trying for the second time, third time and so on. With persistence, you will continue to do the same thing over and over again until you achieve complete success. This will make you an expert in whatever task you are doing.

2. Being persistent will motivate you to try harder. Being persistent means you will keep trying again and again. With every attempt, you will inch closer to success. It will motivate you to put more effort to get closer to your goals when you see that there is an actual difference between where you stand right now, and your previous effort. Self-motivation is an important aspect of being successful.

3. Persistence is a sign of being ambitious.

Only those people who are highly ambitious can

incorporate persistence into every aspect, every little thing that they do in their daily lives. When you keep attempting something with persistence, everyone around you will look at you as an ambitious person. It will build a positive personality image for you, a key in shaping the outlook of a successful persona.

4. Persistence will set a good example to your associates and peers.

A reason why persistence is the key to success especially in workplaces is the reason your colleagues and subordinates will be inspired by your level of persistence. When they see you achieving your goals with determined persistence, they too will try to imitate this trait. This will result in an overall boost in productivity and efficiency for your team, making persistence a highly regarded personality trait in any workplace.

5. Persistence teaches you the value of success

Are you under the false notion that success can be achieved easily by manipulative tactics? Do you think that success can be easily bought? Do you think that success comes with just a little bit of effort? If you have these untrue thoughts in your head, persistence will teach you that success is not that easy to achieve. As you keep attempting to achieve a goal over and over again, you will understand the true value of success. It will enlighten you about the amount of hard work and dedication required to make something happen, preparing you to give your best shot at everything in life if you want to be successful.

6. Persistence will help you gain experience

Being persistent means getting up after a failure, learning from your mistakes and trying again. This whole process will help you gain experience, which is vital if you want all-rounded success. The Multiple numbers of attempts at the same thing will help you find out the things that can go wrong, the things that are crucial to a process or the things that are not required at all. This experience, which was a result of persistence, will teach you stuff that books and procedure manuals don't.

7. Persistence will make you aware of your

weakness

To be successful, you need to be aware of your weaknesses and your faults. Your weaknesses will only be exposed when you analyze your failures and try to find out the things you lack to accomplish something. This is only possible if you are mentally prepared to accept failure, try again, fail again and keep trying until you iron out all your weaknesses to finally succeed. This is why being persistent is the key to success. The most effective words for a lifetime of achievement, success, fun, happiness, joy, and fulfillment: "Keep going. Keep going towards the light, your goals, towards the promise of so much goodness that awaits you. With joyous feelings, hope in your heart, and a song on your lips keep going and receiving achievements, success, love, friendships, fame, fortunes and all else you had imagined. See the pure white light beckoning you, find your path through whatever comes in the way and keep going.

## Persistence-The State of Mind

Success is something we all wish for, isn't it? Undeniably, those who attain great things are those who don't know when to give up. Whether you wish to achieve something or want to lose a few pounds or any goal that you are willing to succeed in, you need to be strong and persistent. Indeed the most successful people in the world have the key quality of perseverance which makes them assume impossible actions to be possible. How many of you can claim with confidence that you have applied persistence and consistency in your everyday life with some measure of success? I think the majority of us dream of incredible things but just lack persistence or the willpower, to follow through to accomplishment. People give up too soon as they have the wrong expectations of themselves and the results. They expect the mode to be easy, and they are amazed when they find the reality to be contradictory. Their enthusiasm quickly melts and they quit. What does being willpower and persistent mean? It is a cliche to simply say "don't give up".

One of the best illustrations persistence is the state

of mind and sustained effort necessary to induce faith. In other words, it exemplifies that determination mixed with Persistence backed by the desire makes a strong tool to ensure the achievement of the goals". The meaning of the term persistence is the quality that allows an individual to continue doing things even if it is tricky or opposed by other people. This is not something someone does with external goals; however, it is something someone does internally. Perhaps we all are aware of the fact that in the face of pain, anguish, suffering, and defeat; it may not be easy to stay persistent. In simple words, persistence means the personality and attitude trait of working harder and harder and trying again and again until success is achieved. Abraham Lincoln is a leading example of persistence and strong willpower in action. Known as one of the renowned presidents in history, Abraham lost 8 elections before he, in the end, became president. He also lost his fortune when he starts losing his business twice and could have chalked himself up to being a loser, but he didn't. However, he didn't lack his determination and believed he could achieve his dreams. If you are passionate about something, chances are you're determined to move towards that activity or thing. It is the quality that motivates people to do things however difficult or unpopular they may be.

## *Chapter One*

### *Keep going until you are successful*

The conventional definition of persistence is: "not letting go or refusing to give up; persevering persistently; firm or obstinate continuation in a course of action in spite of trouble or opposition." It is a developed state of mind much like grit. It is the trademark of achievements since persistent persons push through difficulty, anguish, and pain which refers to the setbacks and roadblocks when pursuing an objective. As the significant component of self-discipline, determination and persistence also provide its own inspiration and motivation. You become more enthusiastic to do something incredibly when your activities started showing results. For instance, when you want to lose all those extra pounds and start exercise and to workout, you will be more enthused when you lost

20-25 lbs and your present wardrobe starts fitting loose Persistence can conquer almost any challenge. When you turn your mind to something and are eager to do everything it takes, by putting in the time and adjusting your plan to get there, you will eventually know the supremacy and power of determination. Some of the major factors or symptoms of lack of persistence are indecision, not being clear in what you want, lack of proper planning, weak desire, fear of criticism, feeling of insignificance and lack of going all out. You may not be fine at doing something for the first time but you will get better and better at it when you keep trying and believe in yourself for the second time, third time and so on. With persistence and consistency, you will continue to do the similar thing over and over again until you accomplish complete success. This will make you a proficient in whatever job you are doing. You have to believe that your victory is guaranteed and no obstacle will stand your way.

Billionaires and political leaders had failed several times and have thought of giving up college but they finally come out ahead as big winners. Edison also made more than 10 thousand experiments before he accomplishes something in making the first talking machine. As the primary factor of self-discipline, persistence also provides its own motivation. You become enthusiastic to do something when your actions started showing great performance and results. Courageous persistence is the main factor than any other that can promise success. And success is somewhat we all want, isn't it? But to be victorious takes persistence. Whether you want to lose your extra fat, get an A in a class, or any goal that you want to succeed in, you need to be persistent. It is the difference between a successful result and a failed one due to giving up.

Perseverance has other names — determination, persistence, a can-do attitude. When getting starting on your vision for success, first and foremost you need to identify your desires and wants. It is when you know the way; you can get a source for inspiration and keep yourself encouraged next, figure out how to achieve what you want? This makes it easier to attain it. Make your objectives actionable every day and follow through. All your objective-setting and planning will go to waste if you won't be able to build up discipline and good habits. Be positive in your work that you will attain what you want. Perseverance separates the losers from the winners. Those who persevere understand that luck is something only failures believe in. Success in life depends on your motivation to never give up, even when the reward is delayed.

How to stay persistent?

Like all states of mind, persistence is based upon specific causes. Take a piece of paper and write down a life goal, what you desire, and answer the questions; what is your definite purpose. Knowing what one longing for is the former and, perhaps, the most important step toward the growth of persistence. Strong motive forces can easily overcome many hurdles of our life. Similar questions like why do you want to accomplish this goal? How will it profit you and the more essential, how will it benefit others? In order to survive your purpose, you have to keep the focus on why you want this purpose/ goal or what the positive results will be in your life? We do have to keep in our mind that our purpose in this world is also to add value to others. If your wishes focus on your own gratification you will sooner or later fail or die a lonely miserable life.

All successful people who have attained great things in their life did so through both willpower and persistence. Even when they failed, they got encouragement and kept going. But we all know that staying determined and persistent is difficult. In any conversation of the qualities of the most successful people, it is always declared that Persistence is one of the, most significant factors in success. Major success rarely comes easily or without an enormous deal of attempt. Often the only distinction between those who succeed and those who do not is the capacity to keep going long after the break has dropped out. It is comparatively easy to persist when things are going smoothly and we see progress, however, great persistent people have found several means to keep going in spite of major setbacks and a lack of confirmation that they are driving near toward their goals.

Some of the significant things that persistent people have in common that keep them moving on long after so many people have given up:

**Visualization for success**

Persistent people have a vision or goal in mind that encourages and drives them. They are often visionaries and dreamers who see their lives as having a high purpose than simply just spending their life. Their vision is deeply entrenched, and they concentrate on it continuously and with great energy and the state of mind. They often think of this dream first thing when they wake up and the last thing prior to they go to bed. Accomplishing this goal becomes the crucial and focal point of their life and they dedicate a major portion of their time and energies towards attaining it.

- **Unshakable self-confidence, self-belief**

Those persons who defeat the hurdles and accomplish greatly are often illustrated as "marching to the beat of their own drummer." Persistence people know what they wish for and are seldom swayed by the view of the masses. To have the perfect intelligence of who they really are, allows the persistent to carry on without being seriously affected by what others think of them or, being appreciated, or being understood by those around them. At the same time as that inner confidence gets shaken, but never gets shattered and continuously acts as a source of courage and strength.

- **Inherent passion to succeed**

There are so many inspiring Entrepreneur and Industrialists who always speak, "If you really desire to do something, you will surely discover a way. If you do not, you will find an excuse." Persistent people never look for any excuse. What keeps persistent people going is their potent level of desire. Repeated failures, losing periods and dead ends, when it seems like no progress is being made, often come before some breakthroughs happen. Persistent people with high will-power have the intensity, state of mind, and inner energy to keep them motivated and going through these hard-hitting times.

## • Talent to Adjust and Acclimatize

Persistent people have the capacity to acclimatize and adapt their action plan. They do not stubbornly persevere in the face of indication that their plan is not running but look for enhanced ways that will increase their probability of success. The motivated and persistent see their life journey as a bunch of dead ends, adjustments, and deviations, but have total faith they will reach their final objective. They are not attached to their ego and are rapidly willing to admit when something is not working. In addition, they are fast to adopt the fresh ideas of others that have been shown to work well.

## • Key success habits

As someone truly said, "Motivation is what gets you going ahead. Habit is what keeps you going."Highly persistent people know it is very tricky to stay constantly motivated, chiefly during hard and the most difficult times and when it appears that no development is being made. They have come to rely upon their self-developing and discipline habits they can count on to carry on the path toward their ultimate goals. They believe the results of the hard work they make today may not be seen for a longer time, but they strongly believe that every single thing they do will count toward their end results.

### • **Commitment to acquire new skills**

Persistent people understand the worth of any objective and reaching will take attempt, time, and constantly learning new skills and thoughts patterns. They welcome fresh ideas and change and continue searching for means they can incorporate these into their lives. Ongoing learning is seen as part of a continuous process through which the highly persistent continually expand the range of tools that they have to work with. Naturally curious type persons not only see learning as a way to reach their objectives more quickly, but they also see self-learning as a way of life. Learning and constant growth do not end at a certain age or phase of life, but they are the spirit of life itself, and thus never-ending.

## • **Role models as mentors and motivators**

While it may come into sight that highly persistent people act without help and don't require any person, most have carefully chosen peoples they follow and admire. These can be individuals who are truly involved in their lives as guides or they can be figures who they have read about and who have extremely impacted them. Such people are often misunderstood on the grounds that they can make those around them feel uncomfortable. The ingrained models assist motivated persons to maintain and motivate themselves in an atmosphere that is not always kind and supportive.

The winners' circle defines persistence as refusing to give up when faced with opposition or hardship. It could be expressed as simply as trying again and again until you keep scoring at sports, maintaining relationships or succeeding at work or businesses. The greatness that you have, the greatness of the condition, is not calculated by what is accomplished. It is calculated exactly by how many times you pick yourself up and try to accomplish something. Among all of the values and morals we can have, it seems persistence is the consistent element in most people who thrive and succeed, no matter what they are succeeding at. We all seem to understand or know that all popular personalities have persistence in huge quantities. They have to keep their mind strong, keeping the boundaries of patience in order to attain the new records. Yet, you can see persistence all over the place you look, even for the job you get paid to do, so there ought to be something incredible to it. If in case you are evaluating what amount of struggle it would take to give your career a boost up, you might come across in the direction of your own persistence. You need to be clear about what you are determined to achieve. What is the result you are in the hunt for? If you need to gather knowledge or resources, then go get them. Once you have your objective, your plan, and the resources, then goes after it with dedication and enthusiasm. Stay focused every day until you get the outcomes you defined. It is also OK to occasionally get propped up by close relatives, family or friends to keep the required attitude that comes with persistence. Persistence is not about the trouble-free road, even though few people make attaining success look easy. Persistence is about systematic and continued to do something even when there is a good reason to give up. Persistence is about the basic confidence of knowing your vision is the right thing to pursue.

## Make persistence a lifelong habit

Another most significant piece to having the higher persistence level is having support. Sometimes when it came to the list of things we wanted to accomplish personally, having a team of people who were above or on your level made you want to persevere and keep going for your aspirations. It is healthy and nice to have a supportive team like family, close friends, relatives, religion and particularly mentors that can be there beside you when you necessitate an additional boost up of motivation. Support from others is always advantageous, but not always simple to find. If you feel like you don't have a mentor or guide in your support team that you could, in fact, talk and sit down to about your aspirations, make an effort to find one, particularly one that has been where you are and who is at present where you are aspiring to go. There is no sense in having a support team that cannot bond and connect to your goals for the reason that they do not have any aspiring goals themselves. You need to evaluate your crowd cautiously and warily. Having a good imagination and thoughts also helps when it comes to persistence. When you can visualize and think about your "dream future" no matter what that might be, these visions every so often can get you through the harsh days. Do not let one failure in your journey of life to success dictate your motivation for the rest of the life. Each and every step is to bring you closer to your ideas and dreams, and when you can clearly notice your upcoming "dream future," you can fully fashion it under your own conditions.

Persistence in the provision of an ultimate crucial goal calls out numerous other virtues in you. You will push yourself to further than what is comfortable to achieve your chosen goal. Furthermore, you should know why you desire your goal in the first place. Plus, your way must be bigger than the difficulties and complications. The bigger the way the better the outcomes, Persistent people have a transparent goal or vision in mind that inspires and induces them. Reaching this ultimate goal becomes the central focal point of their life journey and they devote a larger percentage of their time toward reaching it. If we would like to succeed, we have to pay the price. And the way to success is long with a lot of hurdles and obstacles. No wonder most of the people stop at one point or another after running into the obstacle or barriers. Only the handful of people has this special quality to keep moving forward, and these are some people who succeed. Persistence is essential. Persistence is probably one of the most worthy and excellent characters a person can possess. It's the ability to be determined to accomplish something regardless of any obstructions and setbacks. Hence, arm yourself with the right state of mind and the right tactics to overcome failure. Perseverance or Persistence is mainly about the basic optimism of knowing your dream is the right thing to chase. In fact, there is no other way to succeed and achieve something huge but by developing persistence in your life, and here we would also share a few significant ways to develop it.

## Do you believe in persistence?

Aren't you? Persistence is being able to continue a human action until one has succeeded, like winning a race. When you start running, you keep on pushing yourself until you have crossed the finish line. For instance, in special education, having persistence in teaching a kid until he/she has reached their ultimate goal is like a race. You are persistent in helping them reach their destination and don't stop until they have reached their objective. People tend to hold on to their beliefs even when it seems that they should not. Persistence is the tendency to cling to one's initial belief even after receiving fresh information that dis-confirms or contradicts or the basis of that belief. Every single person has tried to change somebody's belief, only to have them obdurately remain unchanged. For example, you may have had such debates concerning the abortion, or evolution.

In the plethora of cases, resistance to challenges to

belie is defensible and logical. For instance, if you have always done well in racing, getting the third position on some race should not lead you to abandon your belief that you are generally good in the race. However, in the handful of cases, people cling to beliefs that logically should be abandoned, or at least altered. There is overpowering evidence that smoking increases the probability of contracting cancer and that exposure to media violence heightens the likelihood of aggressive behavior. Even, some people strongly deny these scientific facts. People expend considerable mental energy to maintain their opinion when presented with facts that prove them wrong. They will concentrate on experiences that support their point of view merely will ignore any experiences, even their own, that give grounds that they are wrong. They will do the same thing with any other kinds of evidence as well.

**Types of Belief of Perseverance**

There are three types of belief perseverance exist

—1) social impressions 2) self-impressions, and 3) social theories. The first kind of belief consists of beliefs about the self, considering what one believes about his skills and abilities, including body image and social skills. The second type comprises one belief about specific others, for instance, a parent or best friend. The third type comprises mainly what one believes about how the world mainly works, comprising how people act, feel, interact and think. Social theory opinion can be either directly or indirectly learned which means that they can learn through experience as a member or they can be taught. In the first case, children inclined to learn what is expected of them and of others merely by observing and by being a participating member of society. They will learn what it means to be a daughter, a son, a woman, a man, and the behaviors that go with these different roles. In the second case, persons are taught what to believe. They may be taught by their parents or at school, at church.

When it comes to attaining your objectives or creating change in your life if perhaps won't be simple. You may have to struggle. It will likely take a longer time period than you expect. It is almost certain that you will have short-term failures and setbacks along the way. Particularly, when it involves developing new skills, forming a new resolution, creating new habits, or learning new concepts. Now, the good news, struggle, setbacks, battles, and short-term obstacles do not have to drain your motivation. They do not have to make you want to quit before you have put in enough effort and time to accomplish your goal. In fact, psychologists who study motivation and accomplishment say it could be just the opposite; as long as you adopt the right path and the right mindset. According to my raids of research through decades, there are two fundamental belief systems, also called as "mindsets," that evaluate how people respond to setbacks, struggle, obstacles, and failure when pursuing their goals. In one mindset, you are most likely to get discouraged and give up on your ultimate goal. In the other, you tend to embrace the battle and struggle, learn from the hardship or hurdles and keep moving forward to attain your goals– you persevere.

## The science of Persistence: Determined Mindset vs Growth Mindset

What do you believe about human calibers, such as intelligence, talent, and creativeness? If you have adopted a "fixed mindset," you view them as traits that you are either born with, or not, and it is not much you can do to alter it. On the flip side, if you have adopted a "growth mindset," you see them as capacities that you can develop through determination, practice, education, and hard work.

How about character traits like grit, willpower, and self-discipline? With a fixed mindset, you believe attributes like these are mostly static and predetermined by your genes and fostering – either you have them or you do not. Through the lens of a growth mindset, you see them as malleable skills that you can prepare, gear up and strengthen over the course of your life (even science also proves this to be true).

In a fixed mindset, people believe their basic attributes, like their intelligence, ability, or talent, are just fixed traits. They spend their time on the piece of writing their intelligence or talent instead of developing them. They also accept the fact that talent alone creates success; without excessive effort. They are actually wrong. On the flip side, in a growth mindset, people believe that their most basic qualities can be developed through dedication, commitment, and hard work. This view creates a love of learning and a resilience that is necessary for great achievement. Virtually all great people have had these calibers. Teaching a growth mindset creates productivity and motivation in the worlds of education, business, and sports. It deepens relationships. When you read Mindset, you will see how.

## Fixed Mindset Weakens Your Dedication

Our mind is a meaning-making machine. Whether you are aware of it or not, you are continuously monitoring what is happening around you, understanding what it means and deciding what to do about it. This is apparently the significant procedure for your survival, but it is also the main driver of all your suffering – particularly when it is molded by the fixed mindset. When you struggle hardship or fail to attain your ultimate objectives, you make that mean something about yourself. In the fixed mindset, this mainly means you are simply not good enough, or that you for some reason do not have what it takes. For instance, have you ever thought or said things like: I'm not creative, I don't have any self-discipline, I have no talent, I'm not good with new technology, It's hard for me to lose the extra pound, I'm shy, I am not athletic, etc. It is healthy to acknowledge your limitations and recognize where you can be doing better in your life. But that's not what's happening in the fixed mindset. Remember, the fixed mindset believes that abilities and talent are mainly fixed and preset – either you have it, or don't. If you have, great. If not, why even why bother to try? You might as well give up, and keep move on to something simpler. Perhaps, this is not the kind of thinking that helped the big personalities like J.K. Rowling and Stephen King become bestselling authors. It is not the kind of thinking that creates motivation to persevere when the going gets tough.

**Growth Mindset Fortifies Your Motivation**

The growth mindset interprets failure and challenging situations much differently than the fixed mindset. Just remember, the core opinion of the growth mindset is that human powers and talents are malleable skills that you can set up and strengthen over the course of your life. The fixed mindset erroneously views your limitations as permanent. On the other hand, the growth mindset understands they are just a starting turning point – guiding stars that tell you where to spend your energy toward professional and personal development. The growth mindset is an antidote to defeatism. It interprets challenge & failure, not as a signal to throw in the towel, however, as a healthy and natural part of human growing and accomplishment.

This might sound like a good old-fashioned or outdated positive thinking, and maybe it is. The difference of opinion is these conclusions are based on 40 years of stringent, scientific research – more than hundreds of studies that all say similar facts. If you want to strengthen your motivation, accomplish your goals and lead a more fulfilling life, you are best served by a growth mindset. You now have a choice with regard to how you interpret struggle, failure, and setbacks. You can interpret it from a fixed mindset as proof that you are somehow not cut out to win. Or you can interpret it from a growth mindset as guidance for where to keep your focus on your efforts toward personal & professional development. Most persistence research on naive theories has focused on beliefs about people and how they feel, behave, think, and interact and other social theories. Examples include stereotypes about teenagers, Muslims, Asian Americans; beliefs about artists, lawyers, firefighters; even beliefs about the causes of poverty, violence or war.

Early belief perseverance studies tested whether individuals often truly cling to unfounded viewpoints more so than is logically justifiable. However, it is complex and tricky to specify just how much a given belief "should" modify in response to fresh and New Testament. One "C Grade" on a math test should not completely overwhelm other years of "A"s in other math classes, however, how much transform (if any) is warranted? There is one clear and apparent case in which researchers can state how much belief change should happen. That case is when the basis of a precise belief is totally dishonored or discredited. For instance, imagine that John tells

Maria that the new team member is not very active. Maria may even meet and interact with the new member for several days before learning that John was actually speaking about a different new joiner. Because Maria knows that his initial belief about new member's intelligence was based on completely irrelevant information, Maria's impression about the new joiner should now be totally uninfluenced by John's initial statement. This, in essence, describes the debriefing paradigm, the primary technique used to study unwarranted belief perseverance. In the first belief perseverance revision using this way, partially half of the research participant members were led to suppose and believe that they had performed fine on a social perceptiveness task; the rest half were led to judge that they had performed badly. Afterward, all were told that their performance had been manipulated by the researcher to see how participant members take action and respond to failure or success. Participants were even shown the paper sheet that listed their name and whether they were thought to be given failure or success feedback. Later, participants had to guess how well they really did and foresee how well they would do in the future on this assigned task or job.

Logically, those in the initial failure and success situations should not differ in their self-beliefs about their future or actual performance on this social perceptiveness job, for the reason that early beliefs based on the fake feedback should revert to their normal level once it was exposed that the feedback was faked. Nevertheless, participants who received fake success feedback constantly believe that they were pretty good at this task, while those who received fake failure comment persistently believe that they were pretty bad at it. Other studies of social impressions and self-impressions have found parallel effects concerning distinct beliefs.

The initial study of social theory persistence used the same debriefing paradigm to find out whether fictitious info about the relation between the personality attribute "riskiness" and firefighter quality could create a persevere social theory. Though, after debriefing about the fictitious nature of the first information, participants at the start led to believe that risky people make finer firefighters and those initially led to believe that high-risk people make poorer firefighters persist in their initial beliefs. At least there are three psychological procedures underlie belief perseverance. One refers to use of the "availability heuristic" for deciding what is most liable to happen. When judging your own power at a specific task, you are likely to try to recollect memory how good you have done on similar tasks in the past, that is, how available (in memory) are past successful versus failures. However, whether you recall more failures or successes critically depends on galore factors, such as how memorable the several occasions were and how often you have actually thought about them, but not inevitably on how often you have failed or succeeded. The second activity concerns "illusory correlation," wherein one sees or remembers more confirmed cases and few disconfirming cases than really subsist. The third procedure concerns "data distortions," wherein disconfirming cases are neglected and confirming cases are inadvertent. For instance, if you are told that a new team member is rude, you are more likely to treat that individual in a way that invites rudeness or discourtesy and to forget instances of politeness. Research also has examined ways to belief perseverance. The most obvious answer, asking people to be unbiased, does not work, nevertheless, various techniques to reduce the problem. The most successful is to get the individual to imagine or explain how the other belief might be true. This De-biasing technique is referred to as the counter explanation.

**Varied Types**

There are three extraordinary kinds of belief

perseverance, viz.

**Social impressions**

**Self-impressions**

**Naive theories**

### Social Impressions

Social Impressions bring up to the beliefs that people have about others. These could be supported on a one-time, previous experience (either positive or negative) that people have about others and shape an opinion, which leads into forming an opinion. These can be formed with just about any individual.

### Self-impressions

Self-impressions mention to the beliefs that we harbor about ourselves. These have to do with our belief about our confidence, athletic skills, body image, academic inescapable, musical knowledge, and the like. This belief system considers both negative and positive beliefs. For instance, somebody might be a good public speaker, however, he/ she has a strong belief that he cannot speak in the public place, and it cannot be shaken in spite of people complimenting him. The mistaken belief like this one can have severe consequences and can lead to a skewed perspective of oneself. On the other hand, an exaggerated view of someone can also lead to problems.

**Naive Theories**

Such impressions are based on someone's belief about how the world works. Naive theories mostly correspond with social theories—the belief about folks, how they behave, think, and interact with others. Naive theories go on to comprise major stereotypes steeped in the society that has to do with the handful of issues about communities, religion, teen, professions, and other beliefs that may even comprise what gives rise to poorness, causes of war, and violence, and the like.

**Chapter Two**

**Keep going until you are successful**

Holding on to set beliefs and speculations based on unwarranted data and in the light of conflicting evidence, demonstrates that conviction persistence exists, as well as that our conviction framework isn't just shaped based on certainties and sensible data, however to an expansive degree on how we feel about ourselves, about others, and about other general theories and hypotheses. Despite the fact that this unwavering belief can help from numerous points of view, most different occasions, it shapes a boundary which keeps us from settling on the correct decisions. Illustration of a similar will be featured in the accompanying area.

**Examples**

**Positive Example-**You're a brilliant cook and individuals dependably compliment you on your dishes. Yet, on one specific event, you happen to burn the sandwich you're cooking; this does not imply that you're an awful cook or that you need to scrutinize your conviction about being a decent cook. For this situation, the belief perseverance has enabled you to restore your confidence in your cooking and continue.

**Negative Examples**-However, there are occasions when belief perseverance goes about as a hurdle. For instance, a man has met with 4 accidents during a span of a month, but, he keeps on trusting that he is a superb driver. Or then again suppose that your companion has been dating a person who treats her badly, and whilst everybody around her can see this and have been revealing to her the same, she basically declines to say a final breakup to him since she trusts he loves her as too, and he will change.

In the two instances, the individual does not take cognizance of anything that repudiates his/her belief system, which at that point negatively affects his life, since he can't take logical conclusion or judgment.

Why Persistence significant in our Life?

Persistence is the essences of accelerating your prospects of being successful in a specific thing or accomplishing a specific objective, and it likewise can assist you with staying motivated and continue striving towards the one long haul objective you want to achieve. For instance, when you first started your company, you most likely had dreams of success and recognition. You were positive that sales were reaching to pour in, and you'd be busy creating a great deal of cash. When you truly operated your company, it most likely dawned upon you rather quickly that hopes, visions, and dreams alone weren't sufficient. Starting a business taught you that being a business owner isn't as simple as you once thought it might be. In fact, it's a great deal of labor with little reward gained at the outset. This is the reason why business failure rates are thus high. Folks merely cannot overcome the roadblocks and demands that accompany entrepreneurship.

The one word that may be used to describe businessperson who succeeds at business ownership is 'persistent'. You need to be persistent if you would like to be ready to sustain your business through the challenges and hurdles of entrepreneurship and sooner or later reap the rewards of a successful business. The truth is that

Entrepreneurship comes with loads of ups and downs. Typically it feels as if you expertise a lot of downs than ups as you're within the early stages of business development. This is often once your mental attitude needs to stay optimistic and tough if you're getting to go through the hardships of constructing your business. If you're presently having a tough time in your business, you'd get advantage from reading some quotes regarding persistence. These quotes can assist you to understand that you simply aren't the sole one who has undergone troubles as a business owner. Others are through what you're presently going through and possibly abundantly worse. But, they still built successful businesses despite their hurdles as a result of they remained to persevere.

The definition of Persistence is once you are desperate to do one thing considerably and not permitting anyone or any troubles stop you for doing it. This definition couldn't be any length suitable which is what the beauty of determination is and why it's therefore vital for anyone to have. With zero determination, it can lead you to give up on the single thing that you just needed to try to due to the issue that you just faced with or what somebody else has same. Nobody ought to ever surrender on one thing that they really need to try to as a result of everybody can achieve something if they are willing to place in the work a strong mindset towards overcoming the particular challenge and overcoming people that disagree and create trouble and don't have your best interest to your life.

Why Persistence is significant than planning?

We are mysterious creatures. Anguish and hope can coexist and still create something astonishing. Perseverance is the ability to maintain action despite your feelings. It has a lot to do with your life's success and business success. It is considered as an omnipotent. An American politician Calvin Coolidge once stated "The slogan "press on" has solved and always will solve the troubles of the human race". Intelligence and ability cannot take the place of persistence. The worth of persistence comes from a visualization of the future that is so compelling you would give approx anything to make it factual or real. Persistence of action draws closer from the persistence of vision. When you are specifically clear about what you want in such a way that your vision does not change much, you will be more unfailing and persistent in your dealings. Hence, that consistency of action will produce consistency of outcomes. One favorite quote state that "no plan survives first contact with the enemy." We have learned this reality time and time again. Mike Tyson put it well when he stated, "Everybody has an arrangement until the point when they get punched in the face." Regular arranging is basic to maintain a business yet we find that readiness and steadiness are significantly more imperative that the most ideal marketable strategy. Clear emergency courses of action were basic for mission achievement.

Here are reasons that being well-prepared and persistent to tackle life's obstruction is significant than trying to manage things out of your control.

Things do not generally go as planned, thus be ready when the inevitable obstruction or hurdles stand in your way. Whether you are the team member of the big-giant corporation or an entrepreneur growing a start-up, you have probably noticed that plans can change, and change often. But the enterprise has to be well-structured to remain dynamic, robust and strong. Good leaders must continue focused on what lays ahead for foreseeing potential blockage and adjust accordingly. Experiencing letdown along your path to accomplishment does not mean you failed. Failure generally occurs when you allow those experiences cause you to give up. Planning does not ensure adaptability In the Teams, while doing fight dive training we had a saying, "Plan your dive, & dive your plan." Things can get confusing underwater in pitch blackness, however, when you start second guess yourself, it can snowball uncontrollable. That's why it is said, good old fashion common sense is also a great reserve and stand-in when your plan starts falling apart.

For companies, they must have robust financials, nimble leadership, and a team with a shared sense of purpose. Planning does not identify unknowns.

Persistence and obstinacy are what makes companies successful. The character is built during the third and fourth shots at attaining the goal. Not the first try. In trade, there are always myriads of things out of your control like the economy or your client's financial situations. But that's senseless reason to irritate and make kneejerk decisions. You just have to stay calm, cool and positive and try to keep moving. A great quote about persistence from Martin Luther King Jr. states that "If you can't fly you run if you can't run you walk if you can't walk your crawls. But no matter what, you keep moving forward."

Good plans are valueless without proper implementation. Plus flawless execution takes some practice. You can use up all the time in the world developing big plans for your business but if you do not brag the ability to perform on those plans you will surely fail. There also has to be buy-in across the board for organizations to be effectual at hitting their goals. Never discount the significance of having a proper plan and even better contingency strategies. But you need to keep in mind that if you spend proper time to make sure you have the capability to adapt as required, it won't feel like you are trying to steer a cruise ship when an iceberg placed in your pathway. It is perseverance that keeps you moving forward, having important goals are not achieved overnight, they necessitate, and no they demand patience, perseverance, and persistence. If you persistently take action, you will build momentum. "If Columbus had ever thought to turn back, no one would have blamed him. No one would have memorized him either."


In the face of challenge, perseverance ensures that we continue to take action towards the accomplishment of our objective. As World's famous educationalist points out, this may require us to frequent adjustments to our tactics, until we achieve the objective.

"If you have an important point to make, don't try to be subtle or clever. Use a pile driver. Hit the point once. Then come back and hit it again. Then hit it a third time - a tremendous whack."— Winston S. Churchill

Reflecting on your objectives…


• Do you require amending the strategies you are using to archive your goal?

• Have you persevered toward your objective? Or have you perhaps given up too soon?


There are two mentalities: buckle down and achieve your objectives, or not bother since you likely won't succeed in any case. In spite of the fact that this may appear to be an oversimplification, we think this oblivious choice has an aggravating impact all through your life. In the event that you are in the camp of "making a decent attempt leads to achievement", you invest more energy, you take rejection in your stride (despite the fact that regardless it harms), you get up every single time you fall, and you feel motivated to attempt and attempt and try again until you succeed. Whether it's a spelling bee or beginning your own organization: trusting you can accomplish something through diligent work is a critical element for success. Be in the other camp of "you won't succeed" paying little heed to what you do, there is an unequivocally negative example. You feel that whatever you do throughout everyday life, you presumably won't succeed in any case, so you don't feel inspired to attempt in any case. When you confront difficulties and hurdles, you see that as a sign that you will fail. When you are rejected, again you feel weak, powerless and unfortunate.

In psychology, there's an idea called "locus of control": an individual's conviction about how long they can control the events around them: do you take control of the things you can control, or do you blame external components for your prosperity or disappointment. Sooner or later the vast majority have most likely identified with both camps. However, we imagine that over the time goes there is a huge exacerbating impact, encountering little hurdles and difficulties and after that success, which inspires you to handle bigger challenges and to feel well prepared for greater misfortunes.

Set your psyche to an objective, something that

you believe is bizarre and afterward buckles down to accomplish it. Depending upon the "challenge" you pick – it might take the number of hours or only a week. Learn a language, run more distant than you might suspect you could, and figure out how to cook another dish, get the courage to complete an open talking in Public, climb a mountain, build something, influence something, and create something. Set an objective that scares you a little and drives you out of your comfort zone. The truth is that you have accomplished something that you thought was unimaginable and not possible, you will be raring to go for your next toughest challenge and more resilient to the hindrances that you will unavoidably face out and along the way.

Here are 4 reasons Perseverance is vital to your prosperity and success:

## 1. PERSEVERANCE HELPS YOU CONQUER THE UNEXPECTED

At the point when things don't work out as expected, it's tempting to surrender. We lose our confidence and consider moving onward to something that is less demanding. This is actually what the vast majorities of people do on the grounds that we're anxious about disappointment or failure and evade far from things that are hard and necessary. Plans make us feel safe, yet be prepared when things turn out of your control so you can land on your feet. You may need to change course and adjust somehow. Your objective continues to be the same as before, however, your roadmap may need to be changed. Try to develop a nimble mentality by attempting to anticipate potential misfortunes and have an alternate course of action for them.

## 2. PERSEVERANCE ENABLES YOU TO KEEP FOCUSED

At the point when things turn out badly, it is difficult to keep up motivation and core interest. Perseverance enables you to stay concentrated on long haul objectives so you can change your behavior accordingly. Regularly, this expects you to hold feelings in line to keep emotions in check from sabotaging your endeavors and efforts to continue advancing and moving forward. Visualize yourself achieving your objective regardless of what it takes. Watch out for the objective and see yourself reaching the end.

## 3.    PERSEVERANCE    IS    FED    BY ENCOURAGEMENT AND SUPPORT

At the point when things turn out of your control, discover support and encouragement from people around you whom you trust and respect. In view of their experience and ability, search out their recommendation, suggestions, and proposals on the how to proficiently continue moving ahead. Successful individuals with perseverance comprehend that still need to do the tough work, yet it is extremely encouraging when you are surrounded with positive back up. We in our own island as a whole need other individuals' assistance and support. It may be a short talk or a couple of words of assistance. Be the individual who connects when you require assistance rather than to surrender. Do not be afraid to share your situations with other people, however, be particular about it. Ensure they are individuals who really need what is best for you and will give you both valuable and positive feedback. Seek for "mirror" companions or friends who will be fair, cherishing, honest, and objective.

## 4. PERSEVERANCE MAKES YOU DIG DEEP DOWN

If you are on a path that has meaning, value, and significance for you, you are unquestionably on the right path, so keep going. If you are not, then a delay or failure will be enough to make you surrender and try something else. Success can be exceptionally misleading on the grounds that frequently it is the place we remain, regardless of whether it's what truly fills us or not. It is a success that is based in complacency because we are too scared of failure to pursue the type of work that would offer worth and meaning. Don't take the easiest path, dig deep down where it counts and discovers the things that you can't leave. When you are pursuing that sort of objective, it won't make any difference what other individuals say on the grounds that your inner vision is far stronger than any external hindrance you will come up against.

Taking everything into account, in short, persistence is an essential piece of life. Its isolates the complete from the incomplete and just to recap, here are the 5 key reasons why having perseverance satisfies:

• Most successful persons have failed in any event once

• People jump at the chance to test you on the determination

• What comes effectively typically isn't justified, despite any potential benefits

• Knowledge isn't picked up without ingenuity and persistence

• The more you accomplish something, the better you get at it

Permanence, perseverance, and persistence in spite of all obstacles, discouragements, and impossibilities: It is this that in all things distinguishes the strong soul from the weak.


Our mind is incredibly powerful (lot more than you imagine) and with a bit of guidance and mind training, you can completely change your frame of mind. What this actually states is that you can pin down all those magical moments that you have stopped noticing while you hunt after the clock, which, unlike you, by no means has to make any stops. Just try to believe in yourself. You cannot uncover beauty outside if you cannot see it inside yourself. If you are always seeking outward approval you are seriously going to lose precious time. And that is the time you could have spent dreaming about your upcoming big projector or developing any new skill you want to be trained. When you start believing in your abilities and yourself, the possibilities become never-ending. You turn into an imaginative and inspired human being, you dare to grow, you dare to dream, you dare to share your dreams with other people, and you lose your terror of being ridiculed for it. Planning. Education. Desire. All these start contributing to your success part but none of them are sufficient without persistence. – Michael Josephson. Everything starts with a vision, an idea, or yes a dream. The dissimilarity between people who believe in themselves & people who do not is that the people who do believe they will be able to take one step ahead than their strength permits them. And that's when the miracles come into view and they end up triumph no one thought they ever could. "Magic believes in yourself, if you can do that, you can make anything happen." -Johann Wolfgang von Goethe- So, try to get yourself moving. We're all the makers of our own lives. We can act in a lot of dissimilar ways and influence the situations we find ourselves in, and how we take action in all these times will lead to a convincing result.

So it's significant to know what mental state you are in when you are about to take steps. If you are acting from a place of love, understanding, care and, compassion, your actions will surely be graceful, magical, and influential and they will also be part of a better life. When you act out of love you won't very soon feel better, however, you will also inspire other people to do it too. Love always attracts extra love, and that goes way beyond the real results of any action on its own. But if your trials of actions come from your ego, if they have a basis in mistrust, criticism, terror, or suspicion, you'll just attract those similar things. You'll attract a similar type of situations and people over & over again. Now it is the time to change that. Don't be frightened. There is magic waiting for you around the corner, and the finest part is that you can create it. Actually, we have already gone into so many ingredients to create magic, now it's in our hands to magnetize it.

Here are some of the significant things that helped you keep going that day and bring the magic of persistence in your life when everything in you wanted to quit. If you find yourself in circumstances where you want to stop or give up, these lessons can help you, too.

1. Ignore others- At the beginning of the mountaineering, you can only see the people passing in front of you. Every time you see someone hiking without extra effort, you might feel bad about yourself. But when you stopped comparing and stopped worrying everyone else's journey to your own, you seriously began to concentrate on your own mission and how you are going to attain it. As you work toward your vision, it can be simple to get distracted when you see others attaining their objectives faster, easier, far better than you. It can make you feel unsatisfied and disappointed with your own progress. But when it comes to vectoring a goal, what's happening with others is extraneous when it

detracts from your capability to move forward. When tackling a hard task, you need each ounce of energy you can muster. Just ensure to channel it to the right place that will propel you forward.

2. Become your own biggest follower- When you start climbing, you weren't alone. But within 10 minutes, you could be behind and alone. At first, you might be frustrated your companions abandoned you in your time of need. But then you could realize your burden was not theirs to bear. Even though it can be energizing to have others around to encourage and assist you, having them there is a luxury, not a necessity. That lesson allowed you to turn inward and find in yourself the strength, persistence, and willpower to keep going. You began to encourage and high-five yourself with every single step. Sometimes on the path to victory, you have to walk alone. If you find yourself in that similar position, just find a way to give yourself what you need to carry on.

3. Try to appreciate the small things- You began the trek before the sun was up. As you continued to mount, it started to peek around the mountain, giving glimpses of the sparkling beauty all around

you. It could be miraculous. During the catch-your-breath breaks, you marveled at the privilege of seeing the natural world in all her beauty. In those moments, you gave no thought to your struggle. You could be too busy being gratifying for being right there. It can be simple to focus all your energy on reaching your ultimate objective. But if the only thing you can see is your end purpose, you will miss the beauty of the trip along the way. The new experiences and welcome surprises give you much-required fuel to keep going.

4. Focus on the next step- It can discourage you to think how far away you are from the top. So you might reframe your vision into mini-milestones that made the next steps more manageable. Simply take one more step, you thought. OK, now simply get over to those tough stones. And yes once you get to that the track you can stop and rest for a few minutes. When your objectives seem too big, it can feel impossible, which opens the path for resistance to creep in. By breaking your goal into bite-sized pieces, you can keep yourself in motion, persistence and build momentum.

5. Lastly, you can try avoiding your watch- Before the trek; you read that there are so many people make it to the top of the mountain in about 45-60 minutes. But it took you so long. When you focused on the time it was supposed to take, you might get frustrated at yourself for not being fast or good enough. But no one cared how long it took me to hike and get to the top and you should not have, either. All that mattered was finishing your journey. As you work on accomplishing your goals, stop looking at the clock. Stop calculating yourself against something or somebody else. It will only serve to distract you from concentrating on what you require to do right now to advance.

6. Stop looking for a way out- Not everybody who goes to mountaineering or hikes. You can easily take a bus straight to the top & save yourself the physical and emotional tension. Early on in your climb, you might think about retreating or waving down the bus on their way up. When your pain is at the forefront, it is normal to want to make it go away. However, when you spend time seeking a way to abort your journey, you waste valuable energy that could be used to help you conquer

momentary pain and distress for long-term growth.

7. Acknowledge your limitations- You had to be honest with yourself. You were having difficulty getting air and you could not keep the pace of the group. Simply, pushing your body to the limit by trying to keep a speedy pace was not going to work for you. Your path needed to be diverse, and that's OK. After implementing your new tactic, the journey was less exhausting. Your path to success might not look like everybody else's. That's OK. Everybody's situation is poles apart. Instead, acknowledge where you are, so you can offer yourself what you require to be thriving. As you work to attain your objectives, there will be obstructions, bumps, blockages, and bruises along the way. When the journey becomes more painful than what you are used to, it can be simple to throw in the towel & retreat. However, if you follow these lessons, you can find the power to keep going in the midst of complexity. And when you persevere, you will discover the reward was worth the effort. Just so not give up.

As you grow old, you realize that there are real-life strengths that push you to be successful in life and your preferred career and profession.

Our mindset is incredibly influential (lot more than you imagine) and with a bit of guidance and mind training, you can completely change your frame of mind. What this actually states is that you can pin down all those magical moments that you have stopped noticing while you hunt after the clock, which, unlike you, by no means has to make any stops. Just try to believe in yourself. You cannot uncover beauty outside if you cannot see it inside yourself. If you are always seeking outward approval you are seriously going to lose precious time. And that is the time you could have spent dreaming about your upcoming big projector or developing any new skill you want to be trained. When you start believing in your abilities and yourself, the possibilities become never-ending. You turn into an imaginative and inspired human being, you dare to grow, you dare to dream, you dare to share your dreams with other people, and you lose your terror of being ridiculed for it. Plan and desire start contributing to your success part but none of them are sufficient without persistence. – Michael Josephson. Everything starts with a vision, an idea, or yes a dream. The dissimilarity between people who believe in themselves & people who do not is that the people who do believe they will be able to take one step ahead than their strength permits them. And that's when the miracles come into view and they end up triumph no one thought they ever could. "Magic believes in yourself, if you can do that, you can make anything happen." -Johann Wolfgang von Goethe- So, try to get yourself moving. We're all the makers of our own lives. We can act in a lot of dissimilar ways and influence the situations we find ourselves in, and how we take action in all these times will lead to a convincing result.

So it's significant to know what mental state you are in when you are about to take steps. If you are acting from a place of love, understanding, care and, compassion, your actions will surely be graceful, magical, and influential and they will also be part of a better life. When you act out of love you won't very soon feel better, however, you will also inspire other people to do it too. Love and affection always draw towards extra affection, and that goes way beyond the real results of any act on its own. But if your trials of actions come from your ego, if they have a basis in mistrust, criticism, terror, or suspicion, you'll just attract those similar things. You'll attract a similar type of situations and people over & over again. Now it is the time to change that. Don't be frightened. There is magic waiting for you around the corner, and the finest part is that you can create it. Actually, we have already gone into so many ingredients to create magic, now it's in our hands to magnetize it.

Here are some of the significant things that helped you keep going that day and bring the magic of persistence in your life when everything in you wanted to quit. If you find yourself in circumstances where you want to stop or give up, these lessons can help you, too.

1. Ignore others- At the beginning of the mountaineering, you can only see the people passing in front of you. Every time you see someone hiking without extra effort, you might feel bad about yourself. But when you stopped comparing and stopped worrying everyone else's journey to your own, you seriously began to concentrate on your own mission and how you are

going to attain it. As you work toward your vision, it can be simple to get distracted when you see others attaining their objectives faster, easier, far better than you. It can make you feel unsatisfied and disappointed with your own progress. But when it comes to vectoring a goal, what's happening with others is extraneous when it detracts from your capability to move forward. When tackling a hard task, you need each ounce of energy you can muster. Just ensure to channel it to the right place that will propel you forward.

2. Become your own biggest follower- When you start climbing, you weren't alone. But within 10 minutes, you could be behind and alone. At first, you might be frustrated your companions abandoned you in your time of need. But then you could realize your burden was not theirs to bear. Even though it can be energizing to have others around to encourage and assist you, having them there is a luxury, not a necessity. That lesson allowed you to turn inward and find in yourself the strength, persistence, and willpower to keep going. You began to encourage and high-five yourself with every single step. Sometimes on the path to

victory, you have to walk alone. If you find yourself in that similar position, just find a way to give yourself what you need to carry on.

3. Try to appreciate the small things- You began the trek before the sun was up. As you continued to mount, it started to peek around the mountain, giving glimpses of the sparkling beauty all around you. It could be miraculous. During the catch-your-breath breaks, you marveled at the privilege of seeing the natural world in all her beauty. In those moments, you gave no thought to your struggle. You could be too busy being gratifying for being right there. It can be simple to focus all your energy on reaching your ultimate objective. But if the only thing you can see is your end purpose, you will miss the beauty of the trip along the way. The new experiences and welcome surprises give you much-required fuel to keep going.

4. Focus on the next step- It can discourage you to think how far away you are from the top. So you might reframe your vision into mini-milestones that made the next steps more manageable. Simply take one more step, you thought. OK, now simply

get over to those tough stones. And yes once you get to that the track you can stop and rest for a few minutes. When your objectives seem too big, it can feel impossible, which opens the path for resistance to creep in. By breaking your goal into bite-sized pieces, you can keep yourself in motion, persistence and build momentum.

5. Lastly, you can try avoiding your watch- Before the trek; you read that there are so many people make it to the top of the mountain in about 45-60 minutes. But it took you so long. When you focused on the time it was supposed to take, you might get frustrated at yourself for not being fast or good enough. But no one cared how long it took me to hike and get to the top and you should not have, either. All that mattered was finishing your journey. As you work on accomplishing your goals, stop looking at the clock. Stop calculating yourself against something or somebody else. It will only serve to distract you from concentrating on what you require to do right now to advance.

6. Stop looking for a way out- Not everybody who goes to mountaineering or hikes. You can easily take a bus straight to the top & save yourself the

physical and emotional tension. Early on in your climb, you might think about retreating or waving down the bus on their way up. When your pain is at the forefront, it is normal to want to make it go away. However, when you spend time seeking a way to abort your journey, you waste valuable energy that could be used to help you conquer momentary pain and distress for long-term growth.

7. Acknowledge your limitations- You had to be honest with yourself. You were having difficulty getting air and you could not keep the pace of the group. Simply, pushing your body to the limit by trying to keep a speedy pace was not going to work for you. Your path needed to be diverse, and that's OK. After implementing your new tactic, the journey was less exhausting. Your path to success might not look like everybody else's. That's OK. Everybody's situation is poles apart. Instead, acknowledge where you are, so you can offer yourself what you require to be thriving. As you work to attain your objectives, there will be obstructions, bumps, blockages, and bruises along the way. When the journey becomes more painful than what you are used to, it can be simple to

throw in the towel & retreat. However, if you follow these lessons, you can find the power to keep going in the midst of complexity. And when you persevere, you will discover the reward was worth the effort. Just so not give up.

As you grow old, you realize that there are real-life strengths that push you to be successful in life and your preferred career and profession.

- Creativity
- Charisma
- Physical abilities
- Cognitive control
- Artistic talent
- And even charisma

So, the harsh truth that most of us countenance at some point in our lives is that we are not the strongest, prettiest, smartest, fastest, or most talented person in the room. Does that mean you are doomed and will never outrageously succeed in your career? No, not at all. It does mean that you need the perfect plan and strategy that doesn't depend on innate talent to carry the day.

There is hope- Some of you know that you are remarkably talented, gorgeous, superstars, super genius. If so, you do not need any advice and you do not need anybody's help. You are already ruling the earth. Go in peace, follow the magic of persistence my friends. Now, for those who are still in search and want to know the secret, rest assured: there is hope for the rest of your life. Perhaps there are few among us who will admit that they are in this group of hope conception. You may not always be the most talented, smartest, and most imaginative person in the room. However, you can tap into these three superpowers and still attain great success in your life, love, and career.

You simply need to be:

- Consistent
- Resistant
- Persistent

You just do not mean to have persistent, resistant, and consistent traits. You also need to exhibit heroic levels of each. But, the great news is that anybody can do this if they are truly ambitious, dedicated, willing, and as stubborn as famous personalities like Steve Jobs.

- **Consistent**

You create new habits easily and you are consistent with those habits. James Clear has an excellent story on this. Process beats goal sets. Systems will hit vision. Try to concentrate more on what you will consistently do each day and you will achieve more than dreaming about what you want. As people fall in love with planning and goals, and then they get discouraged when things went wrong (as they always do in the end). Or, they want the outcomes, but they really do not want to constantly put in the hard work required. Fall in love with the everyday procedure and enjoy the journey. The outcomes are a side effect. They are nice, of course. It is fun to celebrate the victories along the way. The truth is when you truly start loving the process you will tolerate the hard times and setbacks. The failure here or there does not destroy you. You become overcharged and persistence work as bulletproof. Keep on, move on and you cannot help but see great results.

"We are what we repeatedly do. Excellence, then, is not an act, but a habit." —Aristotle

- **Resistant**

Resistance is the right word for "extremely stubborn." If somebody tells you that you cannot do anything, you should prove them wrong by doing it. Maybe you will even do it twice (like mundane events). If somebody tells you that you must do something, it fuels your willpower and drives to never do that thing. But, more often than not, it may push you or enable you to accomplish things that shouldn't have been possible for someone like you. Or, at least that is what you were told. I was told that I was too poor to go to college.

How many times has someone told you that you weren't good enough to do something? It wasn't because they are willing to spend their lives that way. Just follow the magic of persistence and resist anyone who tells you what you can and can't do with your life. They do not have an idea or know the drive or fire that you have inside. They do not completely understand what you are capable of doing if you persevere. They don't have to live your life. Only you have to. So, "Don't let others define you. You define yourself."—Ginni Rometty

- **Persistent**

"We don't get a chance to do that many things, and everyone should be really excellent. Because this is our life"—*Steve Jobs*. When you are trying to solve a problem or learn something new, you should refuse to give up. You get tunnel vision and you can persist until you get it done, one way or the different ways. Daniel Goleman would call this "Grit" and he considered that it is the biggest predictors of your success. It does not for all time mean that the solution needs to come from me. Sometimes it means that you hire or take assistance from someone who can provide you the solution. But, you should persist until it is done. Just be stubborn, try the magical persistence and refuse to give up or be stopped. This is a magical superpower that only a few have. But now you can easily try and can do this! Anybody can be persistent, set their sights on something, and keep grinding to make it happen. You do not fully agree with every aspect of but, you can believe in the philosophy of persistence.

"Nothing in this world can take the place of persistence. Talent will not: nothing is more common than unsuccessful men with talent. Genius will not; unrewarded genius is almost a proverb. Education will not: the world is full of educated derelicts. Persistence and determination alone are omnipotent."— Calvin Coolidge

You might have a boatload of knowledge, talent, skills, and experience. Everybody does, in their own approach. But, don't worry if you are not the absolute best at everything. Be consistent, persistent, and resistant. Those superpowers are accessible to all of us. Inherent talent can only take you so far. However, the big three will take you the rest of the way. *Permanence, perseverance, and persistence in spite of all obstacles, discouragements and impossibilities: It is this that in all things distinguishes the strong soul from the weak.-Thomas Carlyle*

Persistence is where you get mental strength. Perseverance and determination will carve you as a leader in your industry. It makes you extraordinary and separates you from normal people. You must learn to cultivate a habit of persistence since everything is possible if you persevere. The persistent man or woman does not accept defeat, he just keeps climbing on it. It has incredible magic and power. To reach the zenith tower, if we took one step at a time and continue to take slow and steady steps and not stop. People of greatness have finished the race for success while encountering all the hurdles that are hurled their way, which generally deters common people. Perseverance is a crucial step on your path, to reach your dream. People, in order to live to his fullest potential, must have a vision. To reach that goal you must build your own route. The first step is willpower and the second is dedication, the third is the positive attitude and the fourth is discipline, and the final step is the most imperative being persistent. "Some people have greatness thrust upon them. Very few have excellence thrust upon them." --John W. Gardner

The individual with determination and persistence will succeed over the person with extra talent, more money or higher education. Nothing can replace perseverance not talent nor education, neither genius. Lack of persistence is a weak spot which filters all the way through a majority of the races. Persistence can turn hardship into greatness. Read Autobiographies and Biographies of famous personalities. Follow some of the principles they had engaged to succeed. You can make the right choice today. Focus on the kind of result you want to produce. Set the target for this year. Set tools to work with, to attain this target. Fall in love with your dream and discipline your life. Remember all great people started as average human beings but had a passion, dream, persisted, endured, strong-minded, disciplined, devoted and with a positive mental attitude attained their goals. If they can persist, so you can, so embark on to persist.

*Winston Saga is one of the world's leading sales legends. He is also the CEO of Sales and Motivation International. Winston has been acknowledged as a unique and distinctive authority in the field of sales and personal development. Last year International Biography Centre selected him "International Man of the Year" for his outstanding contribution to sales and Service. He has written 100's of articles to magazine, journals and websites. If you're going through hell, keep going. — Winston Churchill*

If you are seriously going to attain excellence in big things, you develop the habit in little matters. Brilliance is not an exception; it is a prevailing approach and attitude.

## The Power of Persistence

Just believe in yourself even others do not. If you are not at the level you need to be, discover a means to make yourself better. "I've failed over and over and over again in my life. And that is why I succeed." -- Michael Jordan. Ever one craves success. But simply waiting for it, however, would not guarantee success and achievement. That is the key reasons why there are so many people fail to attain their goal: They encounter adversity, suffering, and give up. So let's discuss one characteristic required to achieve what you set out to do: Persistence is the blend of powerful desire and determination. Once upon a time, a person named Paul encountered tremendous obstacles like physical punishment, shipwreck, constant danger, etc., but he chooses never to quit. What motivated Paul to persist amidst struggles? He had a clear goal and trusted that his strong willpower would enable him to achieve it. Paul had his eyes fixed on his ultimate purpose, which he so valued that no situation could deter him. At the end of the day, he achieved what had ordained. Just like the Father have great goals for his kids. Striving for anything less will neither accomplish his nor achieve what he has intended in his life. Once your direction is obvious and clear, you should passionately pursue those goals with the strength and proper guidance—especially when hardship and obstacles arise.

Do not give up! It's how you rise from a collapse that truly defines you as a strong person. For instance the Basketball legend Michael Jordan knows a lot about perseverance and determination. Discussing his stellar career he once illustrated that he had lost almost 300 games and had even missed more than 9 thousand shots. On 26 occasions when he had been hand over with the game-winning shot he had flunked, stated Michael Jordan, "I've failed over and over and over again in my life and that's why I succeed." Eventually, the fact is he succeeded because he persevered. He persisted. He wasn't ready to be a quitter. So, no matter how many times he was fouled (and he was considered one of the most fouled players in the sport's history) he got up and kept going. We can all learn from him and his never quitting perception. Persistence truly pays and makes a way out. One historical classic example you have almost certainly heard and encounter before is that of famous personality-Thomas Edison who said that when developing the electric light bulb he hadn't quit and failed—he had just found 10,000 ways that did not work. Thomas Edison was a veritable and most admired quote machine on the subject of persistence. He also said, "Many of life's failures are people who did not realize how close they were to success when they gave up." And, "Genius is one percent inspiration, 99% perspiration." Persistence. Perspiration. Dogged determination. These are important traits that go a long way in the business world. The majority of the entrepreneurs in their journey to ultimate success occasionally stumbles and now and then takes serious falls. But, like Edison and Jordan, they keep on going for the reason that they know that they have to endure rejection and failure if they want to become the finest in their respective fields of endeavor. If they want to come out on zenith level.

Since the earliest days of his career when he started his passion for the game, he might have encountered obstacles large and small. He overcame them all and continues to do so because of the power of persistence in him, which gave him more confidence, personality, passion, and conviction so that he never give up. Often the only obvious difference between losers and winners is persistence. Losers fold their cards when hardship enters their lives. However, winners never ever give up. Believe in yourself and be prepared to get your skates on. According to research around 75-80 % of all sales, for instance, take place between the fifth and twelfth probability of contact. Just think about that. Just think, how many people are willing to ask for the sale fifth, six, seven, eight times or else more? Majority of them give up by that stage. You have to bear in your mind—whether you are trying to make a sale, plan a trip, prepare for the competitive exams, or achieve anything else in life's great journey—that every time someone says "no" it is just one step closer to somebody saying "yes."

Can anyone develop the power of persistence? Of course, they can. It's one of those great abilities that lie inside all of us. You have a mindset and brain to use. You just have to be confident and to take a leap of faith. You simply have to put them into action. It doesn't matter how capable you are, it is not going to get you anywhere in life without perseverance and willpower. Being determined also means being able to develop a thick skin and handle things when it doesn't go your way. Being able to "stick with it" and keep on moving in your journey with the confidence that when one dream ends a shining new dream is just beginning. It is the magic of the cosmos. Being persistent critically means to overcome any fears that might be holding you back. Fear of making blunders, fear of failure, fear of breakdown, and as well as fear of rejection. Make the bold and strong decision to doggedly pursue your goals. It is the only means you will reach your final destination. Being persistent and determined logically means being willing to do extra and do it more often than the average person would. You go to one more meeting. You can make extra efforts. You make that one last business deals or sales call just before finishing for the day. Conduct more research than your colleagues. Take a course that will advance your career. Push yourself to learn something new. Successful people persist in going the extra mile. They never stop dreaming about the next attempt that will take them to the stars. So, being persistent means being relentless. Never give up. Never surrender. The power of persistence will get you the ultimate prize while others fall by the wayside. As a wise person once said, "You may be dissatisfied if you fail, but you are more destined if you never try at all."

Being persistent and determined is the one thing which isolates the champs from the failures. At the point when an individual makes up his or her mind to achieve a specific accomplishment and set their focus toward that path, declining to be stopped, he or she normally gets what they followed. The intensity of persistence, even notwithstanding difficulty, is the true traits of champions. For sure, the individuals who accomplish incredible things are the individuals who don't realize when to stop. From others, they hear insulting comments and critics continually remind them, over again and again, that what they are endeavoring to do, won't work. However, they continue to persevere.

Advice from good-natured companions and alliances to take their misfortunes like a man or lady does not dissuade the true winner in life. Stopping isn't in the vocabulary of success and powerful individuals. Finding another approach to achieve objectives is fine. Searching for alternate paths to a similar destiny is okay. In any case, to the challenge and courage of heart, there is no such reality as stopping. Being relentless is the one thing which isolates the victors from the losers. At the point when an individual makes up his or her mind to achieve a specific feat and set their concentration toward that path, declining to be deterred, he or she typically gets what they followed.

The principle is simple but significant. It has made winners out of many and keeps on doing as such. Apply this principle and you will taste the sweetness of triumph. Live by this principle and you will experience accomplishment again and again. Instruct this experience with other people and you will experience success over and over again. Being in presence works in this principle to perfection. This principle is in pretty much every achievement book ever written. A portion of those who lived by this principle saw its astonishing outcomes, determined to share what they learned, through their compositions. Unfortunately, numerous individuals don't invest in their books to take in a win rule or success principle that is old, but then new, for each time an individual activates the principle, the outcome in that individual's life is new, sweet, and ground-breaking. The principle is simple: know what you need, you will have what you need, and seek after it persistently, until the point when you get it.

Would it be able to be that simple, some may inquire? Is that really the way to progress? The response is a resounding YES. We challenge you to read after those who have accomplished an extraordinary proportion of achievement and check whether they didn't apply this principle. It will be proven genuine that if you are persistent in a good thing, and you decline to stop, sooner or later, what you seek after will find you. "Nothing on the planet can replace Persistence. Talent won't; nothing is more common than unsuccessful men with talent and ability. Genius won't; unrewarded Genius is just like a proverb. Education won't; the world is loaded with educated derelicts. Constancy and Persistence alone are omnipotent. The motto 'Go ahead' has solved and will take care of the issues of the human race." The conventional definition of persistence is: "Declining to surrender or given up; persevering resolutely; firm or unshakable continuance in n a course of action despite trouble or resistance." Is anyone wonder then, that perseverance is the fundamental principal distinction between a successful result and a failed outcome? In that case, it behooves us to build up the essential traits of determination and perseverance.

If you're going through hell, keep going. -- Winston Churchill. What about Colonel Sanders, the founder of Kentucky Fried Chicken? He was a military retiree and had nothing to his name, aside from his mom's chicken recipe formula. So what did he do? He took his old sports wagon out and started driving to many restaurants after restaurant after restaurant. His purpose was to offer the Chicken recipe formula, yet he was turned down consistently, multiple times 1,007 times before he received his first yes. That one yes is the thing that made Kentucky Fried Chicken possible. We keep going with story after story of those who had to be adaptable, imaginative, flexible, and above all persistent regardless of failing hundreds, sometimes a large number of times. You can also learn from Steve Jobs. He's had had movies made about his story, so you are likely more comfortable with the difficulties and challenges he faced in becoming one of the success and wealthiest corporations on the planet. Members of his own board of directors betrayed him out of his own business. He could have enabled this to stop him; but instead, he chooses to come back to Apple and voted back in as the Apple's Chairman. He created the iPhone, the iPod, and the fresh line of Mac Laptops. Businesses today are incomprehensible without your iPhone.

The three great essentials to achieve anything worthwhile are, first, hard work; second, stick-to-itiveness; third, common sense." -- Thomas A. Edison

A standout and the most essential qualities for all

of us to develop is the ability to persevere through life's difficulties and obstacles. It is very significant to constantly be aware of that EVERYTHING COUNTS throughout our life. Every single action you take daily either rewards you somehow or harms you. Everything either takes away or adds up. Everything either adds to your prosperity or moves you far from it. Nothing you do is unbiased. And all achievement is, at last, the triumph of perseverance. The Power of Persistence helping you to skips once more from difficulties and inspires you to become unstoppable toward accomplishing your objectives.

Stage 1 to getting into the magic of Persistence is to know where you are today and in addition know where you need to go. At the end of the day, shooting darts in the dark and seeking for the best is equal to living your life without clear objectives. Try not to stress if your objective seems unrealistic. Before the Wright Brothers, it was out of mind to feel that a man could fly in a plane. What's more, before yesterday December 8, 2007, a sophomore has never won a Heisman Trophy. It's safe to say that if you can vision it; want it bad enough; and willing to sacrifice and persist, almost anything is achievable. Step 2 is to make peace and harmony with the fact that you will face one obstruction after another to achieve your objective. Some goals are short-term and can be accomplished in a while or in a year. Other objectives might take a lifetime to accomplish. In either case, you will continue to face hurdles and you need to prepare yourself to meet them head-on with self-belief. You need to ACCEPT that they'll be there. How could it be another way? No person is all-knowing, so misfortunes and setbacks are BUILT INTO our life's path.

Stage 3 is to persevere and defeat every obstruction en route UNTIL you achieve your objective. The energy and drive to persevere under the harsh situations is the thing that separates the individuals who make it to the end goal. At the point when obstacles show up...you must PERSIST. When you don't know which approach to turn...get help and PERSIST. And most importantly, if you ever think that you're defeated find an approach to continue onward and PERSIST. Furthermore, Help and assistance for the most persistent people wonderfully seem to appear from some of the most unexpected individuals and places at the opportune time. Persevering people simply appear to figure out how to step forward and prop up when circumstances become difficult. The history books are loaded with these motivating stories.

Obstructions are tough. They knock you down. But they are not intended to KEEP you down. They are intended to revitalize your will, your boldness, your confidence, and your energy. Anyone can succeed and do well staying strong with the breeze at their backs. But what about when the when the wind is at your face and you end up ON your back? As Tiger Woods said in regards to the terrible days, "you have to find it within yourself to get it done." Researchers have discovered that individuals that define obvious objectives for themselves, and decline to stop, will bounce back from any from any misfortunes and accomplish

MOST of their objectives. At the end of the day, you can accomplish any objective you set for yourself as long as you fight till your last trail, and decline to allow the inevitable difficulties and frustrations to dissuade you from your course.

**Find the Power of Persistence**

**Here are suggestions for achievement in any field, and some other objective you strive for everyday life:**

- Be determined.
- Be stubborn!
- Do not take no for an answer.
- Be single-minded.
- Learn from your mistakes—widen your horizons.
- Don't limit yourself. You may need to take a major move to get the start you need.
- Seek out every single chance.
- Read as much as possible.
- Never think you aren't good enough.
- Develop a set of connections and leverage

it.

- Seek out new experiences and environments, and chiefly anyone with a wealth of experience.

- Collect a few qualifications (a degree, maybe an industry certificate) but then make it a priority to collect contacts and experiences, too.

Take time right now to assess your own circumstances and determine your next point of convergence for increasing your persistence in financial matters. Whatever your big, recent accomplishment, select a new one slightly larger and requiring a longer time commitment. Then lay out your plan and get started. Plan now to keep repeating this process, congratulating yourself occasionally for your growing ability for persistent work, until consistent work on all your goals is naturally kept up with ease. In this way, you will experience the power of persistence for yourself.

## ABOUT THE AUTHOR

Positive Thinking Mentor Author Gautam Sharma(gautamsharma.contact@gmail.com)-an intelligent, accomplished, capable, creative professional was born in India, has lived in Asia, Europe, Africa and now living in USA embodies and edifies positive thinking, power of optimism and is sharing insights into human behavior and human potential through philosophical, psychological perspectives with the view of sharing mankind's centuries-old wisdom plus proven, research findings so as to empower people worldwide. The author plans to utilize his strengths of professionalism, wide, varied experiences, creativity and communications' skills to publish the Empowerment Series on improvement, self-help topics. Thank you valued readers for your continuous support, contributions and your favorable feedback. Wishing everybody abundance of positive thinking and better living through the power of optimism.

## OTHER BOOKS BY THE AUTHOR

https://www.amazon.com/POSITIVE-THINKING-OPTIMISM-Original-English-ebook/dp/B01HRY684S/ref=asap_bc?ie=UTF8

also

https://www.amazon.com/SELF-CONFIDENCE-ESTEEM-HAPPINESS-SUCCESS-ebook/dp/B076VM1MNR/ref=tmm_kin_swatch_0?_encoding=UTF8&qid=&sr=

and

https://www.amazon.com/JOY-forHEALTHY-HAPPY-LIVING-Empowerment-ebook/dp/B078L6Y1YM/ref=sr_1_5?s=digital-text&ie=UTF8&qid=1515281796&sr=1-5

Discover your full potential: The Universe within

Gautam Sharma

(Dedicated to valued readers, especially those who appreciate the Empowerment Series books and have written positive reviews)